4/16/74

THE INDESTRUCTIBLE SOUL

THE
INDESTRUCTIBLE
SOUL

The Nature of Man and Life after
Death in Indian Thought

Geoffrey Parrinder

Professor of the Comparative Study of Religions
University of London

London

GEORGE ALLEN & UNWIN LTD

RUSKIN HOUSE   MUSEUM STREET

First published in 1973

ISBN 0 04 281001 9 hardback
       0 04 281002 7 paperback

Printed in Great Britain
in 11 point Fournier type
by Unwin Brothers Limited
Old Woking Surrey

Contents

1 Introduction: the Quest for the Soul

From what IS NOT lead me to what IS
From Darkness lead me to Light
From Mortality lead me to Immortality.[1]

For thousands of years Indian thinkers have concentrated their studies upon the nature of man and, with very few exceptions, the different schools of thought have agreed that there is an inner self or soul in man, and that it is eternal and indestructible. The *Upanishads* and the *Gītā* agree that the soul is

> *Unborn, eternal, everlasting, primeval,*
> *It is not killed when the body is killed.*[2]

Whether such statements are true or false, outdated or of abiding value, must be of great importance to thinking people in any country.

Indian attention to this psychology has been agelong and distinctive. It has been said, with some exaggeration, that in the West study has been directed towards nature, in China towards society, and in India towards psychology. Or Indian philosophy has been regarded as belonging to one great stream of religious thought, parallel to another which was that of Hebrews, Christians and Muslims; but while the Bible and the Koran emphasized the greatness of God the Indian scriptures gave more time to the nature of the soul, a subject that was neglected in early Biblical religion. These are generalizations and a great deal was also said in India about God or the universal Mind, but the special concern with psychology led to the use of many terms for the soul, self, spirit, mind, consciousness, intellect and so on, for which there are often only approximate terms elsewhere.

In modern times Indian and Western thought, which had hardly met in previous centuries, have come into close contact. Not only have visitors gone from the West to travel or work in Asia, but

9

increasing numbers have come to us from the East. These are not only traders, but yellow-robed monks walk in our streets and a great deal of literature has been made available that was unknown to the West in previous centuries. Many Indian sacred texts have been translated, commentaries on them are printed, and countless books expound their doctrines. Not all the expositions are reliable and the better ones may be expensive or out of print, so that popular but careful restatements are needed.

At the same time there has been a spiritual crisis in the Western world, with a decline of organized religion and its authority. In particular little seems to be said today about the soul, or life after death. This has come about either in reaction against the gross pictures of everlasting torment or bliss which were painted for former generations, or because of doubts about the whole subject which produce only silence. Yet there is plenty of interest still in religion in a wide sense. Societies which deal with the esoteric and occult are popular, their bookshops are crowded, and on a more academic level the comparative study of religions is one of the most popular of modern theological disciplines. In addition to groups which study other religions from books, there are many centres in Europe and America in which immigrants practise forms of Hindu, Buddhist, Sikh, Sufi and other religions. The climate is favourable and the need is great for a clearer knowledge of what Indian thought has to contribute to our understanding of the nature of man.

It might be objected that Indian philosophy is pre-scientific, in the Western sense, and so it is outworn or inappropriate. Yet it is the result of centuries of investigation into the nature of man, and is deeply knowledgeable, that is to say scientific. Over two thousand years ago problems were discussed such as begin the *Kena* ('By whom?') *Upanishad:*

> *By whom is the mind impelled and sent out when it soars forth?*
> *By whom is the first breath commanded to go forth?*
> *By whom is speech impelled that people utter?*
> *What is the God that commands the eye and the ear?*[3]

Such questions consider both the nature of the body and the powers that direct it. They are considered from many angles, not dogmatically but critically, and they are discarded if they are found to be unsatisfactory. There is no reason therefore why modern criticism should not be brought to bear upon these problems also, and on the answers that were propounded in India. In the search for truth both old and new methods can be used, but the problems are age-old and are with us still.

The self or soul of man, its relationship to nature, the existence of God or a universal Mind, the survival of death in some form, all of these and related problems are important to thinking men and women in any age. It is not necessary to claim that Indian philosophy always had the right answer to every problem, or expressed its conclusions in infallible statements. That is shown by the variety of teachings which came from the different schools of Indian thought. Endless debates have gone on down the centuries, though in general they have been conducted with mutual respect and tolerance. Yet certain themes have emerged again and again, and others that received less general acceptance may be worth looking at again.

In particular the origin and nature of man received constant attention. This is illustrated in the *Prashna* ('question') *Upanishad*, which discusses numerous questions in turn.

> *Whence are creatures born?*
> *How many powers support a creature?*
> *Whence is the breath of life born?*
> *What are the elements that sleep in a man?*
> *What are those that stay awake?*
> *What is the power that sees dreams?*
> *Whose is this happiness?*
> *On whom are all these founded?*[4]

In modern times contact with Christian and Western scientific thought has produced criticisms of Indian methods and conclusions, but these need not be destructive. Modifications in the expression of even central Indian beliefs, such as reincarnation, may be needed.

On the other hand large gaps in Western thought may be filled, or corrections can be made; for example the notion of God as a Person or Superman, of the soul as a manikin inside the body, of the world as short-lived, in past and future, of heaven and hell in the old symbolism. Both traditional Western and Indian thought can be criticized, but if it is done in a sympathetic and understanding spirit then out of the meeting of the two traditions new appreciation of man and his destiny may emerge.

Further, however, with the modern emphasis that is placed on practical affairs, it might be questioned whether Indian thought can offer much, or whether even that is worth having. These teachings about the soul may or may not be true, but they can appear irrelevant for practical reformers. Politically and socially modern India may seem to be a backwater, if not a vast slum or a potential battlefield for a colossal revolution. It is true that in the past great civilizations have flourished in India, nourished by its religions and philosophies, but the modern population explosion, which so far has defeated plans for social reform, does indeed create such a turmoil that traditional Indian philosophy may become obscured in the land of its origin. Whether this happens or not, Indian thought can now become the inheritance of mankind and it could be preserved outside India if it perished within.

Yet traditionally the relationship of philosophy to social life and culture was close in India. Serious thought about existence was not regarded as an optional extra, or a mental gymnastic, but as fundamental for worthy living. Far from philosophy being unimportant for reformers, it has been considered that activity is blind and unpractical if it is not done in accordance with a proper theory of the meaning and purpose of life. Philosophy is not merely an end in itself, or unimportant for ordinary men, but it is the key to life, in which the meaning of life provides the goal for practical activities. For reformers, and men and women of all classes, the nature of the soul and the purpose of life are of central importance.

The purpose of this book therefore is to present a short and popular study of some of the leading Indian beliefs and theories about man. In such a work unusual names and technical terms must be kept to a minimum, though words from Indian philosophy are becoming increasingly known in the West and enter our dictionaries. Thus the Vedanta system of philosophy is mentioned in the *Oxford English Dictionary*, though the Sankhya system of enumeration has not yet found its place there. Buddhism is well known, but Jainism less so. Brahman is familiar as a term for the divine being; the Atman, soul or self, not so much; and Purusha, spirit or person, hardly at all yet.

References in this book have been kept to a minimum and placed at the end of each chapter. In this way the general reader should be able to follow with ease the presentation of some of the more important Indian teachings on the soul of man, and decide for himself how far they shed light for him on the problems of human existence and destiny.

Indian thought has found expression not only in discussion but also in meditation. It is the result of long examination of the outer world, and constant introspection into the mind of man. It is not just experiment or argument, but apprehension and intuition.

In order that the discussions which are summarized in this book may also lead to meditation frequent quotations have been made from many Indian scriptures. These ancient and often very beautiful verses may be read and memorized, and then their value may be not only temporary but of abiding importance to the reader. In different ways they show that the soul may be apprehended by following various paths, by meditation or by reasoning or by action.

> *By meditation, in the soul*
> *some by themselves may see the soul,*
> *others by reason-discipline,*
> *yet others by action-discipline*[5]

REFERENCES

Quotations have been taken from many books, though most often from the *Upanishads* and the *Bhagavadgītā*. They are usually in my own version, but translations that can be recommended are in R. E. Hume,

13

The Thirteen Principal Upanishads (1921); W. D. P. Hill, *The Bhagavadgītā* (1928); F. Edgerton, *The Beginnings of Indian Philosophy* (1965); R. C. Zaehner, *Hindu Scriptures* (1966).

1 *Brihad-aranyaka Upanishad* 1, 3, 28
2 *Katha Upanishad* 2, 18; *Bhagavadgītā* 2, 20
3 *Kena Upanishad* 1, 1
4 *Prashna Upanishad* 1, 3; 2, 1; 3, 1; 4, 1
5 *Gītā* 13, 24

2   Eternal Nature

Nature in Production

> *Nature is not produced [evolved] . . .*
> *Spirit is neither producing nor produced.*[1]

So declares the third verse of an ancient and important text. The name given to Nature is Pra-kriti, 'making before'; it is the original and primary substance and source of all things. It is Matter as distinguished from Spirit, though opinions differed as to how separate they were. A subtle distinction had already been made in the previous verse between primeval Matter, which is called the Unmanifested, and developed forms of Matter, which are Manifested. In its primal form Nature is eternal and self-existent, and all things evolve or are produced from it, except Spirit which is self-subsistent.

In this teaching, which is only one of many Indian schools of thought, there is a clear distinction between Nature and Spirit, or Matter and the Soul, which are two different orders of reality. They are both real, without beginning or end, and continue for ever. Nature is not produced or evolved from anything else, but it is in a state of perpetual movement in each world eon, and it produces all creatures. Spirit, by contrast, is beyond all movement, causation, time or space. Like male and female principles, Spirit and Nature exist side by side yet differ in constitution. For Spirit, like Nature, is not produced from anything else, but, unlike Nature, it does not produce anything.

Nature has no beginning or end, and in its state of rest it is the Unmanifest. But from its primary state of rest in due course it evolves and becomes Manifest in twenty-three productions or evolutes, according to this theory. First to emerge from Nature is Mind or Consciousness (*buddhi*), which is also called the Great

15

One. From this come the Ego, which is the apparent centre of personality, and from the Ego comes the Reason or Understanding. Then in turn there emerge the five senses: sight, hearing, smell, taste and touch. These are distinguished from five corresponding organs of sense: eye, ear, nose, tongue and skin. Parallel to the latter are five subtle elements: form, sound, odour, taste and tangibleness. Finally there are five gross material elements: fire, ether, earth, water and air.

Because of its enumeration of these productions or evolutes this school of Indian thought is called San-khya, 'summing up' or 'enumeration', though other Indian doctrines also enumerate various elements in different ways. The basic text, from which the verse at the head of this chapter is taken, is the *Sankhya-karika* ('verses'), of about the third century A.D. In the Sankhya system the elements of manifested Nature amount to twenty-three. But there are twenty-five categories in all, for Nature itself is counted as first or second, and Spirit as first or last.

Because of the evolution of all the manifested categories from Nature, and their sole existence in it, some writers have suggested that the Sankhya system is a form of Idealism, similar to those European doctrines which maintain that material objects have no real existence and consist only of ideas. But for Sankhya the external forms have an objective existence, though it is not eternal and in time they will disappear to leave Nature alone with Spirit in a state of rest.

The Sankhya text goes on to say that when Nature has produced the twenty-three evolutes, it finally absorbs them again while Spirit looks on inactive.

As a dancer stops dancing when she has displayed herself to the audience, so Nature ceases producing when she has displayed herself to the Spirit. Generous Nature, endowed with Qualities, without benefit to herself, causes in many ways benefit to the Spirit, which has no Qualities and gives no benefit in return.
I believe that nothing is more modest than Nature, who says, 'I have been seen' and does not show herself again to the view of Spirit.[2]

Nature has Qualities, constituent elements or attributes which run through all its productions, like the strands of a rope. Spirit has no Qualities or attributes, and it is colourless and motionless. But when Nature has first produced its twenty-three categories in the manifested world, it then absorbs them again, showing itself to the Spirit and then hiding itself again. Other views on Spirit or Soul, and also on the body, will be discussed in due turn, but here we may note the parallelism of Nature and Spirit in important schools of Indian thought, and it will also be seen later how this parallelism or dualism was modified in other schools.

Yoga and the Lord

The Sankhya system makes no reference to God, neither to a Supreme Being nor to the minor gods of popular Hinduism. It does not deny God, so it is not formally atheistic, nor is it materialistic, since both Spirit and Nature are eternal. But there appears to be no need in the Sankhya system for a special Creator, and its view of a constant flux, with Nature quiescent and then productive, resembles in some ways the 'steady-state' theory of modern physics. A similar thought is found in a ninth-century poem of the Indian Jain religion:

> *Know that the world is uncreated, like time itself, without a beginning or an end, and it is based on the principles of life and rest.*[3]

In the development of Indian philosophy, however, very important changes were made to the basic Sankhya pattern. The practice of Yoga, a word related to the English 'yoke', and including the meanings of yoking together and yoking by discipline, was very ancient. Its philosophy became worked into a system by the second century B.C. in the scripture of Yoga Sentences (the *Yoga Sutras* of Patanjali). This text was more interested in the practical aim of salvation by disciplined activity than in metaphysical theory, and it accepted the pattern of Nature and Spirit taught by Sankhya.

But if there was still no Creator, Yoga found it necessary to introduce the worship of God or the Lord in the search for perfection.

The Lord [Ishvara] is a special type of Spirit, untouched by suffering,
works [karma], or the result of works or impressions.
In him is the highest knowledge of everything.
He was teacher [guru] of the ancients, and is not limited by time.[4]

This Lord was added as twenty-sixth to the categories enumerated in what is now called Sankhya-Yoga. The Lord was a sublime spirit as a model of perfection, an object of devotion, a help to meditation and concentration, though he was not God in the fullest sense.

Vedanta and the Divine

Sankhya and Yoga are counted as two of the six schools of orthodox Hindu philosophy, though they were both critical of the ancient orthodox Vedic scriptures and rituals, and the Sankhya text in its second verse says that the revealed or scriptural means of ending misery are linked with impurity, destruction and excess. It has often been debated where Sankhya and Yoga arose, with arguments ranging from the view that they developed out of the *Vedas* and *Vedanta*, to modern theories that they were survivals from the ancient non-Aryan or Dravidian religion which flourished in the Indus plains from about 2500 to 1500 B.C. The outward forms of this civilization were destroyed by Aryan invaders from central Asia, but the religion and philosophy may have survived and come to flourish in later popular Hinduism. Possibly the Jain religion, which also spoke of Souls (see next chapter), and Buddhism, which appeared to deny them, likewise were derived from non-Vedic sources.

The *Vedas*, from a root meaning 'knowledge' (related to the English 'wit'), were collections of hymns to the gods of the Aryan priests and warriors who came into India from 1500 B.C. These texts were not written down, but preserved by great feats of memory for centuries, they say little about nature and creation apart from some mythology, yet the *Vedas* came to be regarded as the most sacred of all Indian scriptures. However, Vedic philosophy really began with the *Ved-anta*, the 'Veda's end' (perhaps composed from 800–300 B.C.), also called the *Upanishads*, 'private sessions'. Here wise men and women, kings and priests, teachers and pupils, discussed the problems of philosophy: creation, soul, world-soul, sleep, death, life after death, reincarnation, and so on.

In the *Upanishads* spirit and matter are rarely separated from each other clearly, as they are in the Sankhya teaching. Their chief concern is with the human soul and the divine spirit. This will be discussed later, but here briefly it can be noted that the *Upanishads* declare that in the beginning there was soul, or world-soul, that it was true being, intelligent, and one, and from its thought all creatures were produced.

> *In the beginning, this [universe] was just Being, one only, without a second.*[5]

The Gītā and God

The Sankhya philosophy is hardly referred to until the later portions of the classical *Upanishads*, and then only in passing. But it is taken up and developed in the short but greatly influential *Bhagavad-gītā*, the 'Lord's Song', about the third century B.C. Sankhya teaching had probably not developed into a coherent system at that time, before its own basic texts were written, but its principal ideas must have been well known. From its second chapter the *Gītā* refers to Sankhya, but in the sense of 'theory', the belief in indestructible souls. This is contrasted with Yoga, in the sense of 'practice', activity and its discipline, and the *Gītā* often says that Sankhya and Yoga, or theory and practice, are the same or produce the same results.

The *Gītā* says a great deal about the Strands or Qualities of Nature. These natural Qualities operate in all kinds of activity, and all creatures follow Nature. The Lord is introduced as an object of meditation, as in the Yoga philosophy. But soon a change occurs when it is declared that this Lord is ruler of all and unborn, but he consorts with Nature by his creative power (*maya*) and comes to exist in the visible world.

> *Altho' I am the Lord of Beings*
> *with Self unchanged, altho' unborn,*
> *by my own Power I come to being*
> *ruling this Nature of my own.*[6]

Later the *Gītā* says that all beings come out of Nature, which is the Lord's, and return to it at the end of a world-eon, and that God himself emanates this whole host of beings by means of his own material Nature.

> *Into my material Nature*
> *all kinds of beings pass, from when*
> *a cycle ends and when a cycle*
> *begins I send them out again.*[7]

This seems to mean that Nature is used by God and is dependent upon him for reproduction. The sexual imagery of the union of male and female, like the union of heaven and earth which figures in much ancient mythology, becomes plainer still later. In the *Upanishads* the name Brahman was applied to the Absolute Being, or neuter World-soul. But the *Gītā* speaks of Brahman as a mother or womb in which the Father, God, plants the seed. Brahman here is ike Nature (Prakriti) of the Sankhya teaching, but the Lord has become God in the full sense, as activator, sustainer and goal of all beings.

> *Great Brahman is a womb for me*
> *and I implant the seed therein,*
> *out of that comes every being*
> *taking therefrom its origin.*[8]

In this ingenious manner the *Gītā*, with its notably catholic flair for combining very different ideas, turned Nature into the dependent partner of God, like the consorts (*shaktis*) of the gods in Hindu mythology. Nature may still be eternal, but its activation and power depend entirely upon God, whose work in this can be called creation. This is not a 'steady-state' theory, in the sense that nothing ever happens, any more than it is a theory of linear or inevitable progress in a line upwards. The universe revolves in cycles, but the beginning and end of each cycle, as well as the entire maintenance of the world and men, are all dependent upon the power of God.

> *All manifested beings come*
> *from that Unmanifest at day,*
> *dissolving when the night has come*
> *in that Unmanifest, they say.*[9]

Cycles of Existence

Nearly all Indian philosophies believe in successive creations and dissolutions of the universe. The world is not created out of nothing, it has no clear beginning and no final end, but there is an endless process of creation, dissolution and re-creation. In popular mythology the periods of evolution and dissolution were called days and nights of a personal god, usually named as Brahmā (different from the neuter divinity Brahman). In some versions, where the god Vishnu is the Supreme Being, Brahmā arises out of his navel and sets the new evolutionary process in motion. Each day and night of Brahmā lasts a thousand years of the gods, which in turn are twelve thousand human years, so a day of Brahmā is twelve million of our years. The years of the gods are divided into four eons (*yugas*). The first was the Krita which lasted 4,800 years, the Treta lasted 3,600, the Dwapara 2,400 and the Kali 1,800. It goes without saying that we are living in the last and worst age, when religion declines and immorality is rampant, a pessimistic thought that is common to old teachers. With such a concept of the cosmos, the vistas of time are endless, nature is constantly evolving and dissolving, and souls are in an eternal and repetitive journey.

Such a plan of evolution and dissolution, or others like it, lies behind most Indian philosophies. It appears to work automatically, though God as an agent or creator plays a smaller or greater part in it. The Logic (Nyaya) school of Hindu philosophy taught that the end of the world would come by the action of the Lord (Ishvara), not through cruelty but because he wished to give rest to living beings in their suffering. The creative force in all souls and elements would cease to act, the atoms of which all were composed would cease to combine. Material things would disintegrate and souls would remain suspended in an inanimate condition. When in the cycle of eternity God wished to bring about creation again for the good of all beings, he would do this directly, or through the intermediary of a creating deity, Brahmā, combining the atoms again.

One of the later classical *Upanishads* rejects the notion that an inherent nature, or time, could be the cause of the world. God is the creator, and if this means that he must have some Qualities or attributes then that is acceptable.

> *Some sages talk of inherent nature,*
> *and others of Time. Deluded men!*
> *It is the greatness of God in the world*
> *that makes this Brahma-wheel revolve.*
> *He by whom all this universe*
> *is ever encompassed*
> *is intelligent, author of time,*
> *possessed of qualities, omniscient. . . .*
> *Having created this work he rests again.*[10]

Even the Buddhists, who in early centuries concentrated on the practical way to salvation, and regarded as unprofitable the speculation whether the world was eternal or whether it was non-eternal, spoke of creation and dissolution.

> *There comes a time when, sooner or later,*
> *after the lapse of a long long period,*
> *this world-system passes away. . . .*

Now there comes also a time when, sooner or later,
this world-system begins to re-evolve.[11]

At first, it is said, the palace of Brahmā appears, but it is empty. Then some being or other whose span of years is full comes to life in this palace and when others join him he thinks, because he was first, 'I am Brahmā, the Lord of all, the creator.' But the only one who knows the truth is the Buddha, and he is not concerned with speculation but with the path to liberation.

> *That does he know, and he knows also*
> *other things far beyond. . .*
> *the rising up and passing away of sensations,*
> *their sweet taste, their danger,*
> *how they cannot be relied on,*
> *and not grasping after any . . .*
> *he is quite set free.*[12]

Later Buddhism came to consider that there was nothing permanent, all things were changing, and there was no identifiable being. The only possible way of thinking correctly about beings was to regard them as mere appearances, or even as void and emptiness. There was some wavering between a theory that the absolute void was ultimate, and the orthodox Hindu beliefs that something permanent and real existed as the basis for passing appearances.

After many centuries of debate between different religious philosophies in India, there came a great revival of philosophy in the school called Vedanta. This must be distinguished from the *Upanishads*, but it is called Vedanta because these later teachers, from the ninth to the thirteenth centuries A.D., based their teachings on the *Upanishads*, the first *Vedanta*, and on a later work called the *Vedanta* or *Brahma Sutra*, the Vedanta text.

This Vedanta text begins by noting the 'desire to know Brahman', the Supreme Being, and it is defined as the source 'from which origin of this', meaning the universe. On such cryptic phrases the Vedanta commentators wrote many pages to express different

23

views of the nature of the Supreme Being, and his relationship to the universe. But by none of these philosophers was Nature regarded as existing and creating independently of the divine Being. Vedanta differed from Sankhya, which held that Nature existed alongside Spirit as an independent reality. The individual souls postulated by Sankhya were also generally interpreted by Vedanta as being manifestations of the one supreme Soul or Self. This must be considered later, and for the moment attention is directed to some of the closing words in the commentary of the great philosopher Ramanuja on the *Vedanta Sutra*.

> *There is a supreme Spirit whose nature*
> *is absolute bliss and goodness;*
> *who is fundamentally antagonistic to all evil,*
> *who is the cause of the origination,*
> *maintenance, and dissolution of the world,*
> *who differs in nature from all other beings,*
> *who is all-knowing, who by his mere thought*
> *and will accomplishes all his purposes;*
> *who is an ocean of kindness to all who depend on him.*[13]

REFERENCES

1 *Sankhya Karika 3*
2 *Ibid.* 59–61
3 *Mahapurana* 4, 39
4 *Yoga Sutra* 1, 24–6
5 *Chandogya Upanishad* 6, 2, 1
6 *Bhagavadgītā* 4, 6
7 *Ibid.* 9, 7
8 *Ibid.* 14, 3
9 *Ibid.* 8, 18
10 *Shvetashvatara Upanishad* 6, 1–3
11 *Brahma-jala Sutta* 2, 2–3, from T. W. Rhys-Davids, *Dialogues of the Buddha*
12 *Ibid.* 2, 15
13 *Vedanta Sutra* with Ramanuja's commentary, 4, 4, 22, trs. G. Thibaut

There are several popular English translations of the *Yoga Sutras* of Patanjali, and this, with the *Sankhya Karika* of Ishvara-Krishna, can be read in *A Source Book in Indian Philosophy*, edited by S. Radhakrishnan and C. E. Moore, and in part in *Sources of Indian Tradition* edited by W. T. de Bary and others.

3   Indestructible Souls

The Proof of Spirit

> *Because all composite things are for another's use,*
> *Because there must be an absence of the*
> *three Qualities and their modifications,*
> *Because there must be a superintending power,*
> *Because there must be someone to experience,*
> *Because there is a tendency towards isolation,*
> *Therefore the Spirit exists.*[1]

Nature is evident in its visible manifestation, but the existence of the soul needs to be proved, and in the five assertions above the Sankhya text attempts to demonstrate the reality of soul or spirit (*purusha*). Spirit must exist because Nature is composite and exists for use, because there must be some reality beyond the three Qualities of Nature, because there must be a directing force like the driver of a chariot, because someone other than matter must feel and think, and because there is a yearning towards a higher life of abstraction from material gain.

Such considerations lead to the conviction that the spirit exists. Nature is powerful, and evolves all things, but it is blind. The spirit of man is the perceiver and enjoyer of the natural world, though how different it was and whether Nature can rightly be spoken of as distinct from Spirit was a problem much debated by the Vedanta philosophy.

It has been seen that Sankhya speaks of Nature and Spirit as the two original and basic categories in its scheme of twenty-five categories, and this implies a kind of dualism of matter and spirit. But in fact it is a pluralism, because spirit is not one but many. The facts of life show that there are billions of living thinking beings, which are souls or monads, separate units of being, and in recognizing and interpreting this fact the Sankhya teaching is trying to remain faithful to experience. It goes on to indicate this diversity.

> *Because of the separate distribution of*
> *birth and death and individual organs,*
> *Because of the diversity of occupations,*
> *Because of the differences of the three*
> *Qualities in each,*
> *It is proved that there is a plurality*
> *of spirits.*[2]

Each soul is distinct, and yet the argument given here appears to suggest that the spirit is affected by the Qualities of Nature, which was denied in the second of the five proofs given. But it was believed that every soul, which was in itself completely immaterial and unattached, was accompanied by a subtle body (*linga*). This subtle body was formed from the finer principles of matter but therefore it was affected by the Qualities which produce individual differences in all beings.

The Spirit itself was called 'witness', 'isolated', 'neutral', 'seer', and 'inactive'. But its connection with the subtle body made the Spirit appear to be active, instead of passive and neutral as it really is. Nature alone acts through its three Qualities, and Spirit when it is united with Nature experiences but does not act, though it may appear do do so. This thought appears frequently in the *Gītā*, which insists that the true self does not act and so encourages a warrior to fight, knowing that his true self does not kill and cannot be killed. The Sankhya text continues that the Spirit is united with Nature, so that each may help the other.

It is in order that the Spirit may be able to contemplate Nature, yet be separate from it, that the union of both is made, like the union of a lame man and a blind man, and through that union the evolution of the universe proceeds.[3]

The material universe was evolved by unconscious Nature for the use of the Spirit that it might gain a knowledge of material things and through this contrast with itself the Spirit would come to know its difference, as subject from object, and would seek liberation from matter. This is illustrated by a well-known story of a blind man who met a lame man in a forest. They agreed to help each other get out of the jungle, the blind man carrying the lame on his shoulders and the lame man directing their path. Nature is the blind man since it cannot see, and the Spirit is lame since it cannot act, but by their union liberation is gained from the jungle of delusion—for the Spirit. So Nature functions for the liberation of the Spirit.

> *As the unintelligent milk flows for the growth of the calf, so the emanation of Nature acts towards the liberation of the Spirit.*[4]

It should be noted again that the Spirit does not act, and although the common Indian belief in reincarnation or transmigration (see below) is accepted, it is clearly stated that it is only the subtle body which migrates. The Spirit, as a spectator, is unmoved and at ease. It beholds Nature but is not bound to it, and does not migrate, for it is Nature, which has many forms, that is bound or migrates. At the end of a world-cycle Nature returns to its state of quiescence before emerging into another evolution, but the Spirit is ever free and unchanged.

> *By its wisdom, the Spirit as a spectator,*
> *unmoved and at ease, beholds Nature,*
> *which has now turned back from its forms to its primitive state,*
> *because the desire for production has ceased.*[5]

Plural Souls

A similar belief in countless individual souls was taught in the ancient religion of the Jains, so called because their saintly teachers were called Jinas, 'conquerors'. The material universe was a fact not to be explained away, and the existence of countless living beings was also accepted as a fact of experience. The whole universe could be divided into living souls (*jiva*, a term related to the English words 'vivify' and 'quick'), and the non-living (*a-jiva*). The principle of life, which was quite distinct from the body, was this vivifying soul, and it was directly perceived by true knowledge through introspection. The chief characteristic of the soul, as distinct from non-soul, was awareness, and this was a valid proof of its existence.

The Jains believed that there were innumerable souls, which were eternal, and they occupied countless points of space. But against Vedanta view (to be considered later) that all souls are really one, the Jains held that experience shows them to be separate and infinite. So a medieval Jain teacher declared:

> *If the soul were only one*
> *like space pervading all bodies*
> *then it would be one and the same character in all bodies.*
> *But the soul is not like this.*
> *There are many souls,*
> *just as there are many pots and other things in the world—*
> *This is evident from the difference of their characteristics.*[6]

The Jains believed that the soul filled all the body, from the tips of the hairs to the end of the toenails, so that it could feel all sensations. This filling of the body was often described as similar to the manner in which a lamp lights up a whole room when it is in a corner of the room. Further, like other Indian thinkers, the Jains believed that souls were to be found in all living matter, from gods and men down to animals and insects. Although they did not believe in a creating deity, since the universe was eternal, they held that gods and saints were part of the universal system. These beings also transmigrated to other lives according to the results of their actions. Eventually enlightened souls would gain liberation in Nirvana, a state of calm bliss at the roof of the universe. But the place left vacant by the departure of such rare souls would be easily filled by the minute beings which are packed closely into the world like a box filled with powder.

The Soul Indestructible

Belief in the indestructible soul appears often in the *Upanishads* and is fundamental to the argument of the *Gītā*. The first *Upanishad* declares:

> The Soul is 'not this, not that',
> it is intangible, for it cannot be grasped,
> indestructible, for it is not destroyed,
> detached, for it is not attached.
> It is unbound, does not tremble,
> and cannot be hurt.[7]

Many other attempts are made at indicating the fine and subtle nature of the soul. It is of the measure of a thumb ever seated in the heart of creatures. It is like a hair, or the hundredth part of the point of a hair, subdivided a hundredfold, and partaking of infinity. It is not male or female, nor yet neuter. It is hard to see, hidden in the secret place of the heart, dwelling in the depth, and primeval.[8]

The *Katha Upanishad* gives a subtle and rather amusing discussion between a young man who has died and Death himself. After granting two boons to his guest Death is reluctant to give the third, which is a somewhat artificial demand to know whether a man who has died lives again or not: 'What is there in the great passing-on?' After trying to dodge the issue, Death affirms that the soul is never born and never dies, it is not killed with the death of the body.[9]

The *Gītā* takes up this affirmation of an indestructible soul, quotes these two verses almost verbatim, but with a slight change of emphasis. Its problem was posed by the warrior Arjuna in his dialogue with the god Krishna, which occupies the whole of the *Gītā* in one form or another. Arjuna is reluctant to fight in an impending battle and seeks divine guidance. The very first answer given by Krishna to this dilemma affirms the principle that the soul can never be destroyed, quoting two verses from the *Katha Upanishad* but reversing their order.

> He who thinks this a killer
> and he who thinks that this is killed

have neither really understood—
this does not kill and is not killed.

This *is not born, has no mortality,*
came not to be nor ever comes to be;
unborn, eternal, lasting, ancient one,
it is not slain when slaughtered bodily.[10]

The difference between the *Gītā* and the *Katha* is that the latter is speaking of the supreme Soul or Absolute Being in the general manner of the *Upanishads*, whereas the *Gītā* is referring to the individual soul in order to reassure Arjuna that even if the body is killed in battle his soul is immortal. However, in the second verse, in its usual synthesizing fashion, the *Gītā* seems to be combining the two ideas. In an earlier verse it was said that the soul does die and take a new body, and that would refer to the embodied soul of the individual. But there is also soul-in-itself, which participates in or is even identical with the absolute divine being, Brahman, and this cannot be born or die.

This is like the Sankhya belief in the Spirit (*purusha*) which is connected with Nature and reincarnation through a subtle body (*linga*). In fact the *Gītā* admits that this doctrine of the abiding soul is Sankhya theory, and then it proceeds to teach Yoga practice. The *Gītā*, in the first verse quoted above, speaks of 'this' as not being a killer, and the usual word employed is 'embodied self' (*dehin*, formed or moulded, like the English word 'dough'). The same word was used in the *Katha* and other *Upanishads* for the individual rather than the universal soul. This embodied soul can be deluded or led astray by desire, or bound by the three Qualities of Nature, though in essence it is unchanging and can gain immortality by overcoming these bonds.

As a mirror covered with dust
shines brightly when it has been cleaned,
even so the embodied self [dehin]
when it has seen the true nature of the Soul [atman]

31

> *becomes united, attains its end,*
> *and is freed from sorrow.*[11]

The *Gītā* also speaks of the 'life-soul' (*jīva*, the term used by the Jains), sometimes as identical with the 'embodied self', sometimes as a minute portion of the divine substance which is caught up in Nature.

> *Part of Me in the world of life*
> *becomes the eternal living soul.*[12]

The 'Me' here is Krishna, who for the *Gītā* is the supreme and only God, the absolute Being. Although with others, like the Jains, the term for this 'life-soul' was used technically for the transmigrating soul, yet by the author of the *Gītā* it is used more loosely of a part of the divine. Critics, like the philosopher Shankara a thousand years later, asked how the partless Absolute could have a part divided from itself. In logical philosophy this would be impossible, but in the *Gītā* religion is not separated from philosophy, and its religion demanded that God should be infinite and indivisible, and yet have parts of himself in the world and even assume a visible and limited body in an Avatar, a 'descent' or embodiment of the divine.

Another term for the Soul (*atman*) is commonly used for the timeless being or universal soul, and will be considered in the next chapter. However, occasionally even this more universal entity is so identified with the individual that it is born, and develops through eating and drinking.[13] The more usual identification of the wider soul with the universal being, Brahman, will be discussed later.

No-self or Non-soul

An apparently flat contradiction of the belief in an indestructible soul came from the Buddhists, though it is often difficult to know whether they are taking an agnostic position, criticizing the limitations of an argument or denying its claims altogether. Both the Buddhists and the Jains were attacked by Hindu philosophers for their dislike of speculation, and common use of qualification in terms such as 'perhaps' and 'maybe', 'perhaps not' and 'maybe not'.

Sankhya philosophy and the Jains did not believe in a creating god or a supreme Being, though Sankhya-Yoga taught the existence of a special soul as Lord, and the Jains gave more than divine honours to their Jinas or Conquerors. But all these schools and the theistic *Gītā* and *Vedanta*, believed in an indestructible soul. Buddhism went further, ignoring God though adoring Buddhas, but attacking ideas of the soul, and teaching No-self or Non-soul (*an-atta*).

In a sermon on 'the Marks of Non-soul', attributed to the Buddha and probably ancient, statements and answers appear on this topic.

> *The body is not soul.*
> *If the body were the soul*
> *this body would not suffer sickness,*
> *and it would be possible to say of the body*
> *'let my body be thus, or let it not be thus'.*
> *Now because the body is not soul*
> *therefore it is subject to sickness.*[14]

The same statement is reiterated, in the repetitive manner of the Buddhist teachers, about each of the other constituent parts of the body. These are five bodily elements: form, feeling, perception, tendencies and consciousness. None of these is the soul, which by definition should be permanent and pleasant.

> *What do you think,*
> *is the body permanent or impermanent?*
> *Impermanent, Lord.*
> *But is the impermanent painful or pleasant?*
> *Painful, Lord.*
> *But is it fitting to consider what is*

C

> *impermanent, painful, and subject to change,*
> *as 'this is mine, I am this, this is my soul'?*

These statements are negative, and express the Buddhist aversion to speculation, as well as its practical concern with self-denial. Further, early Buddhism was opposed to egoism and insisted again and again that nothing in this passing world can be called 'I' or 'mine' or 'self' This teaching passed over into Hinduism through the *Gītā*, which in its first chapters was much influenced by Buddhism

> *The man who puts off all desires*
> *so that his longing motions cease,*
> *who does not think that 'I am this'*
> *or 'this is mine' proceeds to peace.*[15]

Whether early Buddhists believed in an indefinable soul, a 'soul-in-itself', like other Hindu philosophies, has been much debated. Apparently such a belief would not be excluded by the verses quoted above, which deny that the body and so on are the soul, and which refer to the soul as impermanent and pleasant but refuse to locate it. It will be remembered that the Sankhya school distinguished a 'subtle body' from the eternal Spirits, and the *Gītā* differentiated the 'embodied self' from the unborn soul. Some writers consider that Buddhism does not exclude belief in a universal Soul, but that is not the point at issue here, even if it is unlikely. The question now is whether Buddhist teaching had room for a soul without any distinguishing characteristics yet connected in some way with people in this world. Recent studies of Buddhism as practised, even in the most conservative countries such as Ceylon and Burma, reveal that modern Buddhists, both monks and laymen, think of themselves as having a fairly stable existence and speak of their personal survival in terms which imply belief in something not unlike a soul.

As Buddhism developed in its early centuries spiritual problems were tackled in different ways. An important and popular text is the *Questions of King Milinda* (Menander) which gives supposed dialogues between a Greek ruler of an Indian province and a Buddhist monk called Nagasena. The king took up the Buddhist five-fold classification of shape, feeling, perception, tendencies and consciousness, and since the monk had declared that he was not to be identified with any of these, the monarch concluded that 'there is no Nagasena'. In reply the monk analyses the chariot in which the king had travelled, saying that the pole, axle, wheels, body, flagstaff, yoke, reins and goad are not the chariot and so there is no chariot. Yet it is because they are taken together that a chariot exists as a name. Similarly with regard to the monk:

> *It is because of material shape and feeling and perception and tendencies and consciousness that Nagasena exists as a designation, a term, an appellation and a name.*
> *But in the highest sense, the person is not got at here.*[16]

Another problem for King Milinda, if the theory of a permanent self was held, was the identity of a person throughout the growing stages of his life.

> *Now that you are grown up are you the same as when you were a boy, young and tender and lying on your back?*
> *Oh no. That boy was one thing, I who am now full grown am another.*[17]

But if that is so, objected the monk, the king can have had no parents or teachers, since they too would have changed at each moment of growth. Yet his mother cannot have been completely different in every stage of the growth of the embryo and there must have been some continuity. This was a continuity of mental elements (*dhammas*) which link up the separate moments.

> *A continuity of dhammas runs on,*
> *one rises and another ceases,*
> *it runs on as if there was no before or after.*[18]

It is clear that the Buddhists were strongly opposed to the notion of the soul as a sort of manikin inside the body, or a being in any way identifiable with any of the constituent parts of the body or mind. They encountered difficulties, however, when explaining the nature of rebirth, a belief which they shared in company with all other Indians. If there was no identifiable soul to act as carrier between one life and the next, then it would seem that there was no reason to link the present life with anything in the past. As will be seen later, the Buddhists maintained that the link between lives was Karma, one's deeds, though critics might object that there could be no reason to attach the Karma of one life with another life, if there was no embodied soul involved in the transmission of Karma.

Further, if there was no soul passing from one life to another, then the Buddha himself could not survive death and does not now exist. So Milinda asked Nagasena, 'Is there then the Buddha?' He received the categorical reply, 'Yes', but it was followed by a denial that the Buddha could be located or pointed out.

> *The Lord has attained final Nirvana, in the element of Nirvana that has no basis remaining.*
> *It is not possible to point at the Lord and say that he is either here or there.*[19]

This was very proper, and the text continued with the practical note that the Buddha could be pointed out in the 'body of Doctrine', for this is what he taught. Elsewhere such speculations as to whether the Buddha exists, or non-exists, were called unprofitable, not concerned with true doctrine, not helping right conduct or detachment or purification or quiet or tranquillity or knowledge or insight or Nirvana. Buddhist dislike of speculation and emphasis on practical religion and morality was one reason for its appeal, at least to certain kinds of men and women, though not to philosophers until later developments led to a kind of idealism. But in its teachings on Nirvana and rebirth, as discussed later, Buddhism was probably closer to the mainstream of Indian thought than might appear on the surface. In Buddhist countries to this day the Buddha is worshipped as 'the god beyond the gods', and people speak of 'my rebirth' or 'my last life' as if they were the same person or had a continuing soul.

Even in the ancient texts, while denying a located and identifiable self, there are Buddhist verses which affirm the eternal existence of the indescribable being or state.

> There is an unborn, unbecome,
> unmade and uncompounded,
> for were there not an unborn, unbecome,
> unmade and uncompounded
> then no escape could be discerned from
> what is born, becomes, is made and is compounded.[20]

Alongside different beliefs in, or denials of, indestructible souls were powerful Vedantic teachings of the individual soul (*atman*) and the cosmic soul (*Brahman*) and their union or identification. Strangely ignored by the Buddhists, contradicted by the Jains, modified into personal theism by the *Gītā*, this pantheism or monism came to dominate much of Hindu thought, and the next chapter must be devoted to it.

> He is the unseen Seer, the unheard Hearer,
> the unthought Thinker,
> the not understood Understander.
> There is no Seer other than He,
> no Hearer other than He,
> no Thinker other than He,
> no Understander other than He.
> He is your soul,
> the Inner Controller, Immortal.[21]

REFERENCES

1 *Sankhya Karika* 17
2 *Ibid.* 18
3 *Ibid.* 21
4 *Ibid.* 57

5 *Ibid.* 65
6 *Ganadharavada* 1, 32 f., *Sources of Indian Tradition*, 81 f.
7 *Brihad-aranyaka Upanishad* 3, 9, 26
8 *Shvetashvatara Upanishad* 3, 13; 5, 9; *Katha* 2, 12
9 *Katha Upanishad* 2, 18–19
10 *Bhagavadgītā* 2, 19–20
11 *Shvetashvatara* 2, 14
12 *Gītā* 15, 7
13 *Shvetashvatara* 5, 11
14 *Samyutta Nikaya* 3, 66
15 *Gītā* 2, 71
16 *Milinda's Questions* were fully translated by I. B. Horner in 1964, or in selections in E. Conze, *Buddhist Scriptures* in 1959. *Milinda* 28
17 *Ibid.* 40
18 *Ibid.*
19 *Ibid.* 73
20 *Udana* 8, 3; translated by D. M. Strong, 1902
21 *Brihad-aranyaka Upanishad* 3, 7, 23

4　Soul and World-Soul

Those who discourse on Brahman say,
What is the cause? Brahman?
Whence are we born? On what are we founded?
By whom directed do we live our various conditions
in pleasure and pain, O you theologians?
Is it Time, or inherent nature,
necessity or chance,
the elements or a womb,
or a person as the cause?
It is not a combination of these
because there is the Soul.[1]

Soul and Being

Some of the most influential and subtle discussions of the origins of the universe were given by the thinkers of the *Upanishads*, and these accepted as axiomatic the existence of the soul or spiritual element in man. The Soul or Self in the verse above is *ātman*, a word derived from a root meaning 'to breathe' (it is related to the German *atmen*, 'to breathe', to Greek *atmos*, 'vapour', and so, distantly, to English 'atmosphere'). *Atman* is used in a number of ways, and commonly as a reflexive pronoun for 'oneself', 'himself', and so on. In this sense it is used by the Buddhists, but it does not necessarily mean 'soul' for them.

In Hindu texts *atman* means both the soul in man and the soul of the universe. In the *Vedas* it is used of the vital breath, while in the *Upanishads* the word *atman* is often used about man and 'Brahman' about the universal spirit. In translations some writers render this word as 'soul' and others as 'self', but the latter word may be too individual and associated with the ego, and it may be better to speak of 'soul'.

The *Upanishads* begin with numerous speculations about the origins of things. 'In the beginning', they say, there was nothing, or there was death, or there was *atman*, or there was Brahman.

In the beginning the universe was undifferentiated, but it became differentiated by Name and Form, as people are distinguished by name and shape. And the soul entered into the body to the tips of the finger-nails, and was hidden like a razor in a sheath or fire in a brazier. In the beginning there was only the Soul, which first identified itself by saying, 'I am'. It was alone and wanted a partner, so it made that soul fall into two parts, becoming husband and wife. A similar myth of an original man-woman is told by Plato in the *Symposium*.[2]

Belief in the soul meant that the Upanishadic thinkers held to the supremacy of the spirit or mental element; they could not believe that the world came from nothing, resulting from chance or blind necessity. Nor could they accept the Buddhist view that there was no discoverable soul holding together the material elements of the body, since they thought this soul was fundamental. To the notion that nothingness or non-being came first, before the creation of the world, they returned a scornful denial. So a father taught his son:

> *In the beginning, my dear,*
> *this universe was Being alone,*
> *one without a second.*
> *It is true that some people say:*
> *'In the beginning this universe was just Non-being,*
> *one without a second,*
> *and Being was born from that Non-being.'*
> *But really, my dear, how could this be?*
> *How could Being be produced from Non-being?*
> *No, in the beginning this universe was*
> *Being alone, one without a second. . . .*
> *It took thought,*
> *May I be many, let me procreate.*[3]

By subdivision of the original Being there arose the basic elements of the universe, both the material world and the souls which emerge from Being and return to Being. Like thinkers elsewhere the Upanishadic teachers sought for a unifying principle behind the diversity of the universe. The *Vedas* had sung of many gods, though sometimes seeing that 'that which is One the sages speak of in various terms'. But an important Upanishadic dialogue reduces the number of gods from a supposed 3,306 down to thirty-three, then to six, three, two, one and a half and one. 'What is the one god? Brahman. They call him That.'[4]

Brahman-Atman

The different elements of the universe could be traced back to an original unity, and the many gods might be merged into one, but there remained the difference between divine and human, between God and man, a difference which has remained central in some religions. Yet the Upanishadic thinkers disliked the dualism which satisfied the Sankhya philosophy, or the pluralism of that and the Jains, and they felt that there must be a unity behind this final difference. The unchanging reality behind the passing visible world was called Brahman, and it came often to be regarded as virtually identical with the essence of man, the *atman*.

The term Brahman seems to have developed from words meaning growth, evolution, development, and especially 'holy power'. It was identified with 'vital breath', was used of sacred texts and powerful spells, and was related to a creator god Brahmā, and to the Brahmin (Brahmana) priests. The 'theologian' was the 'brahman-knower'.

In the *Upanishads* Brahman came to mean 'the All', the whole of existence and beyond, both the universe which exists now and the unchanging eternal Being. So Brahman is the divine essence, the source from which beings come, in which they live and to which they return. Brahman is not God, in the personal sense, being 'it' rather than 'he', having no attributes and only to be described in negatives as 'not this, not that'. It is not an object of worship, but of knowledge and meditation. Brahman is the philosophical Absolute, the Unmoved Mover of everything.

These doctrines were not consistently maintained. Sometimes it was held that 'there are two forms of Brahman', the stationary

41

and the moving, the beyond and the actual. On the other hand, Brahman would be identified with everything: 'Brahman before, Brahman behind, to right and to left.'[5]

It was almost inevitable that Brahman should be identified with the *atman*, the World-soul with the individual Soul, and this happened in the *Upanishads*. While some verses distinguish the soul of man from the absolute, others virtually identify them.

> *This is my Soul within the heart,*
> *smaller than a grain of rice,*
> *or a barley corn, or a mustard seed,*
> *or a grain of millet,*
> *or the kernel of a grain of millet.*
> *This is my Soul within the heart,*
> *greater than the earth, greater than the atmosphere,*
> *greater than the sky, greater than these worlds.*
> *Containing all works, all desires,*
> *all odours, all tastes,*
> *encompassing all this universe,*
> *it does not speak and has no care.*
> *This is my Soul within the heart,*
> *this is Brahman,*
> *when I depart from hence I shall merge into it.*[6]

The Soul in the heart is Brahman, which is its origin and goal. It is within, immanent and tiny. It is also transcendent, encompassing and beyond the universe, silent and undistracted. Thus the Soul is exalted to infinite heights, and the divine enters into the smallest places.

The Soul is said to be within the heart, perhaps from anatomical observations of the empty ventricles in the heart. Many metaphors are used to express its nature and activity. In the space within the heart is the lord and king of all, who is unaffected by good and bad actions. Or the body and heart are called the 'city of Brahman', which contains everything, yet when old age overtakes it the Soul remains free from evil, age, death, sorrow, hunger and thirst, for it seeks only Reality. Brahman is also the Inner Controller, who moves and knows all things. It dwells in earth, water, fire, sky, air, heaven, sun, space, moon, ether, darkness, light, beings, breath, tongue, eye, ear, mind, skin, understanding and semen, yet while dwelling in all these things and controlling them it is unknown to them. 'He is your Soul, the Inner Controller, the Immortal.' Or again, this earth is like honey for all creatures which feed on it, but within the earth is the shining immortal Spirit (*purusha*) which is the Atman-Brahman. Similarly with the waters, fire, wind, sun, heavens, moon, lightning, thunder, space, law, truth, mankind and Soul, within them all is the Spirit, the Atman-Brahman.[7]

These long and repetitive descriptions represent teaching and dialogues, but they are based on intuitions, arising from innumerable meditations on the nature of the universe and man. They are not systematic accounts of facts, and they inevitably contain inconsistencies. They feel after the oneness of Brahman, and when the diversity of a natural phenomenon attracts their notice they declare that this also is Brahman, for the differences between objects and beings are simply names and forms. Just as from a lump of clay everything made of clay can be known, the modifications being merely verbal distinctions and names, and as from one piece of metal everything made of metal can be known, for the reality is just metal, so when this Soul is known as Brahman then everything else is known.[8]

Thou art That

If the differences in the outer world can be so resolved, how much more can those between the individual human soul and the divine. In a series of nine examples the sage Uddalaka taught his son, who had received a long education but only in formal religious texts. The father imparted the inner truth, 'whereby the inaudible becomes heard, the imperceptible becomes perceived, and the unknowable becomes known'. Behind the modifications of individual objects there is a single essence or being, and when this is known everything else is known.

As bees prepare honey from different flowers by reducing them to one essence, and as salt is diffused in water to make it all taste the same, so there is unity behind all differences, there is being, soul, and you yourself are that Soul.

> *The eastern rivers flow to the east*
> *and the western to the west,*
> *they go from sea to sea and become the sea,*
> *but once there they do not know*
> *'I am this one' or 'I am that one'.*
> *Even so, all these creatures*
> *though they have come from Being*
> *do not know 'we came from Being'. . . .*
> *That which is the finest essence*
> *the whole universe has it as its soul.*
> *That is Reality. That is the Soul.*
> *That art thou.*[9]

Each of the nine illustrations given to illustrate this universal unity ends with the refrain, 'that art thou', or '*You* are *That*' ('that thou art', '*tat twam asi*'). This famous phrase is one of the 'great words' of the *Upanishads*, the subject of endless comments, and it has been taken as a summary of Vedanta doctrine and even of Hinduism.

This verse means primarily the unity and identity of individual and universal. The inmost essence of man is one with the ultimate essence of the universe. This is the doctrine of non-duality (*a-dwaita*, 'not-twoness'), and it is in clear opposition to dualism or pluralism. As such it has been called monism or pantheism, but these terms need to be distinguished from each other. Pantheism is the doctrine that God, or the divine, is everything and everything is divine, which is not what the above text says. It asserts Reality, or Truth, the universal Self, the underlying oneness. Therefore it might be more properly called monism, the doctrine that only one exists, denying the ultimate duality of matter and mind, as of individual and universal. But it is more than a simple assertion of unity, since it is a unity of Soul, or ultimate spiritual being. So it is a pantheistic monism, or a non-dualism of individual and universal souls.

In criticism of the doctrine of monism, it might be asserted that it is saying nothing, except that everything exists or is the same. It is tautology, saying the same thing again in different words. If there is no distinction of individual and universal, then you are you, or it is it. This is no explanation of the universe or man, but the simplest statement that whatever is exists. It is not a religious statement, or an expression of spiritual truth, since no God or distinctive being is involved.

But such criticism ignores several essential points. The first is that the *Upanishads* are not completely systematic or consistent. They did not so much set out a logical system of philosophy as try to express intuitions of eternal reality. Secondly, other thinkers and commentators who followed were aware of logical and philosophical difficulties and wrote at great length to suggest solutions.

Moreover, although Brahman-Atman is not God, in the personal sense, yet it is considered to be the supreme and conscious reality. Brahman is immanent within man, the Inner Controller, but it is not just identified with human nature, because it is both 'smaller than the small' and 'greater than the great'. It is transcendent as well as immanent. Most especially Brahman is not an inert or blind Nature because it is conscious, it is Mind and Spirit. Although neuter and indefinable, Brahman came later to be spoken about positively as Being-Consciousness-Bliss (*sat-chit-ananda*). The divine was the Supreme Being, the highest wisdom, the most profound bliss.

Hence, the illustration of rivers running into the seas and losing their identity was true as far as it went, but if it was taken to mean that they lost everything then the analogy with the Soul broke down. For in the divine the Soul found its true being. Its limited consciousness became the supreme consciousness without all the limitations of humanity, and so it attained to supreme peace. The liberated soul, which had found its own reality, dwelt in Being-Consciousness-Bliss. More will be said about this later under 'Brahman-Nirvana'.

45

Brahman and God

One important development, in some Upanishadic and later schools, in teaching the supremacy of Brahman, was the appearance of a more clearly apprehensible Supreme Being in response to religious need. If Brahman was the Inner Controller, then it was not difficult to conclude that it controlled everything and stood beyond the world also, ordaining sun and moon, earth and sky.

> *The One who, himself without colour,*
> *by the manifold exercise of his power*
> *distributes many colours in his hidden purpose,*
> *and into whom, its end and its beginning,*
> *the whole universe dissolves—*
> *He is God,*
> *may he endow us with a clear mind.*[10]

The later classical *Upanishads* continue some of the pantheistic themes, but also bring flashes of clearer theism. The *Katha* speaks of the Soul in the heart of creatures, but then asserts that its greatness is perceived 'through the grace of the Creator'.[11] This is a bolt from the blue, which is not explained. But the *Shvetashvatara Upanishad* which follows is much more clearly theistic. From it come both the quotation above and the one at the head of this chapter. It dismisses the notion that the cause of all things can possibly be nature, chance, necessity or time, or a combination of them, because there is a soul, an intelligence that is not explained from material compositions. Then it declares that the ultimate one, though himself without colours or attributes, distributes these to the others and from him the whole universe proceeds. 'It is the greatness of God in the world, by which this wheel of Brahman is made to revolve.'[12]

This supreme God is eventually identified as Rudra, a storm god of the *Vedas*, and especially by his attribute of Shiva, 'kindly'. This is the great deity who to this day commands the worship of countless millions of Hindus as creator, destroyer, yet lover of souls. Combining both the gracious and the harsh elements of

nature, the worship of Shiva is one of the purest forms of monotheism that India has produced. At the same time this *Upanishad*
speaks of Brahman as supreme, hidden in all creatures, yet envelop-
ing the universe.

> *The Supreme, the Great,*
> *who is hidden in all things*
> *according to their bodies,*
> *the One who embraces the universe—*
> *knowing him as Lord men become immortal.*[13]

He is the Inner Soul of all, the witness of all deeds, the one thinker
and controller. He dwells in the nine-gate city, in the cave of the
heart, all-pervading, bountiful and kindly.

This *Upanishad* was followed by the *Gītā*, which quotes it, and
yet, remarkably, the later book ignores Shiva and sets forth Krishna
as the supreme unmanifested One, above Brahman. Although it is
superbly catholic, the *Gītā* is also carefully selective, combining the
Sankhya and Vedantic philosophies, but subjecting them to its
clear monotheism. It also uses the word Spirit (*purusha*, person),
taken from both the Vedic and the Sankhya texts, but in the *Gītā*
indicating the Highest Spirit, the supreme Deity.

In the *Gītā* the divine is partly the 'fixed, still state of Brahman',
the abode of the liberated soul, but it is also identified with Nature
(of Sankhya), into which God places his seed. Brahman is also
sacrifice, and in fact the whole of time and eternity. Yet there is
the supreme God, who is 'the base supporting Brahman', the ground
of everlasting right and unchanging bliss.[14] Or again there is
perishable Nature, including all embodied beings, and imperishable
Brahman.

> *In the world are these two spirits,*
> *perishable and Imperishable;*
> *the perishable is all beings,*
> *the Imperishable is immovable.*

> *But another higher Spirit*
> *is what they call the Highest Soul,*
> *the changeless Lord who enters in*
> *the three worlds and sustains them all.*[15]

The Highest Spirit is God (Krishna) himself, above Brahman, and this most secret word is now revealed to and known by the man who has passed beyond delusion. The solution which the *Gītā* offers to the dualism of Sankhya, and the monism of Vedanta, is the God who is within yet beyond all beings, in whom they abide but who himself is not limited by them in any way.

It is remarkable that the *Gītā*, which knew and quoted the *Upanishads*, never refers to the great word 'Thou art That'. Its nearest approach is to speak of 'That, it is' (*tat, sat*), as Reality and Being, linking them both to practical duty and to eternity.[16] For the *Gītā* the soul is part of the divine, yet though it speaks of 'becoming Brahman', and of the emanation of all beings from the divine, these beings are not identified with the Highest Spirit. In a long chapter (number ten), the *Gītā* declares that the supreme Deity is the chief of all classes of gods and men: he is the soul in all beings, the gods Vishnu and Shiva, the greatness in sages and singers, and he is even his hearer Arjuna. But the reverse is never stated. Arjuna is not Krishna, as he would be on the Upanishadic theory of 'thou art that'. So in a subtle way the *Gītā* contrives to make the best of all worlds, selecting the themes of dominant philosophies. It chooses elements from Sankhya, from Buddhism and from Vedanta, and then displays its own vision of a supreme Spirit in whom all subsist. He is the ruler of Nature, the basis of Brahman, the home of the Soul, and the refuge of the needs, to be served by both sexes and all classes of society.

Non-dualism or Qualified?

The great teachers of the later Vedanta schools (ninth to thirteenth centuries A.D.) wrestled with the problems of the relationships of the individual and the universal souls, and they wrote at great length about them in commentaries on the *Upanishads*, the *Gītā* and the Vedanta text. Shankara (about 788–820) began by affirming the existence of the self, which cannot be doubted since all knowledge depends on self-experience and this is its own proof. The basis of experience is Brahman, which is known as the self of everyone, but although Brahman is indicated by negatives it is not non-being but rather it is the only being, the essence of our world and of the cosmos.

The appearance of the world is attributed to Maya, 'power, illusion, unreality' (distantly related to our word 'measure'). This idea appears only slightly in the *Upanishads*, but it is used by Shankara of an impermanent principle used by Brahman to create the appearance of the world and also the bodily shapes whereby as a personal Lord he appears to his worshippers. The world exists through Maya, it is not non-existence or a Void, but it is not ultimate reality and it will disappear with the full enlightenment and union of the soul with Brahman. Creation, according to Shankara, is not the purposive act of a personal God, for that would imply some desire or limitation on his part, but it is the 'play' of the Lord whose power is unlimited.

Shankara held that the individual soul was really the same as the universal soul, and when it was rid of Maya or ignorance it would lose its limitations and merge into the divine, realizing its own true nature. So the 'great word' of the *Upanishads* was fully accepted, for both scripture and reason prove it.

> *That same highest Brahman constitutes*
> *—as we know from passages such as 'thou art that'—*
> *the real nature of the individual soul,*
> *while its second nature, namely that aspect of it*
> *which depends on fictitious limiting conditions,*
> *is not its real nature.*
> *For as long as the individual soul does not free*
> *itself from ignorance, in the form of duality,*
> *—which ignorance may be compared to the mistake*
> *of him who in the twilight mistakes a post for a*
> *man—and does not rise to the knowledge of*
> *the Self, whose nature is unchangeable, eternal*

D

*cognition, which expresses itself in the form
'I am Brahman'—so long it remains the
individual soul.*[17]

Shankara put forth the fullest expression of monism, rejecting any duality of the soul and the divine which might imply 'I' and 'thou', subject and object. So he is the favoured teacher of all those monistic or pantheistic writers, past and present, who present a Neo-Vedanta as a 'perennial philosophy.'

Shankara also criticized Buddhist teachings as contradictory and absurd since they taught, he said, the reality of the external world or the reality of ideas only or a general nothingness. But he himself has been called 'a secret Buddhist', since his view of the world resembled that of idealistic Buddhists, with the addition of Brahman. But this was a large addition.

Other great Vedanta philosophers, with an even larger religious following, gave different interpretations of the soul and the world-soul. Ramanuja in the eleventh century held that the world and soul are real and not illusions, but they depend upon God and form a unity, since they exist as the body of Brahman. This idea had already been hinted at in the *Upanishads*.

*He who, dwelling in all things,
yet is other than all things,
whom all things do not know,
whose body all things are,
who controls all things from within.*[18]

This is the immortal Inner Controller, and while it is called the Soul it cannot be simply the individual soul of man, since it is said to dwell in the sun and the sky and all things. Ramanuja developed this idea, and taught that Brahman is the soul of the body which includes the world and individual souls. These souls and things cannot exist apart from God, and yet they are never completely identified with him, and Ramanuja pointed out that the 'great word' itself may be interpreted in different ways.

In texts such as 'thou art that'. . .
the words 'that' and 'thou'
denote a Brahman distinguished by difference.
The word 'that' refers to Brahman omniscient . . .
the word 'thou', which stands in co-ordination
to 'that', conveys the idea of Brahman in so
far as having for its body the individual souls
connected with non-intelligent matter.[19]

So Ramanuja taught a 'qualified non-dualism', the communion or union of souls and God, but not their identity with him. This is a fundamental distinction. In full enlightenment, or in the hereafter, the soul would be released from all limiting barriers, but it would not be dissolved into God, since one substance cannot dissolve into another. The soul will always need a God superior to him to adore, as God needs man to be the object of his love.

It is not surprising that Ramanuja was a more sympathetic commentator on the theistic passages in the *Gītā* than was Shankara, who tried to force it into the pattern of monism. Ramanuja taught a belief in a God who could be approved personally, identifying Brahman with the great Vishnu, and speaking both of the love of man to God and the love of God for man. He gave philosophical strength to the many followers of Vishnu, and there followed a great revival of Vishnu devotion, expressed in the flowering of mystical poetry, music, worship and art, in the Indian Middle Ages and widely influential to this day.

The third great Vedanta philosopher, Madhva in the thirteenth century, went even further and propounded a frank dualism (*dwaita*) of God and man. He identified Brahman with Vishnu, who is immanent in the world as the Inner Controller of souls, but he is also transcendent as world-controller. The soul is limited and suffers because of its own Karma, but all souls are different and they find their release by the grace of God and proceed to adore him forever. Madhva admitted that some Upanishadic texts seem to declare the identity of the soul and the Supreme Being, such as 'thou art that', but he rightly pointed out that other texts spoke of God and the soul as separate. A favourite verse, which comes

51

in two *Upanishads*, speaks of two birds on a tree, of which the active one is the soul and the tranquil one is the Lord.

> *Two birds, close companions,*
> *cling to the same tree;*
> *of the two, one eats the sweet fruit,*
> *the other looks on without eating.*

> *On the same tree a person is sunken*
> *and deluded, grieving for his impotence;*
> *but when he sees the other, the Lord contented,*
> *and his greatness, he is freed from sorrow.*[20]

Because of such texts Madhva declared that 'the Supreme Lord is absolutely separate from the whole class of souls'. Since all these commentators paid at least lip service to the authority of the *Veda-Vedanta*, this use of proof texts was justified. But they also tried to support their doctrine by argument, and Madhva held that if there appears a conflict between texts the understanding 'should be guided by that statement which is consistent with reason'. His very rationalism, however, made Madhva less attractive than other teachers, and he has never had the great following that came to the monistic Shankara and the more theistic Ramanuja.

Parallel with the worship of Vishnu, which was promoted by the *Gītā*, Ramanuja, and many others, there has flourished also the worship of Shiva. Supported by some of the later *Upanishads*, there came to be many devotional writers who spoke of the relationships of God and the soul. Among the Tamils of south India, in particular, there was a long tradition of mystical poetry, in texts that have remained popular for temple services as well as for personal use.

God (Shiva) is regarded as both ruling the universe and dwelling in all beings. Non-dualism or monism is rejected, since the love of God for man demands a relationship of lover and beloved, yet the soul comes to a knowledge of its divinity by loving union with God. When ignorance is dispelled, the soul recovers its proper nature and so there is union with God. Yet this union is not identity, since loving relationships with God persist throughout. But this union brings a loss of egoism, for God destroys all thought of 'I' and 'mine', and teaches men to abide in him.[21]

But perhaps the last word on this subject should be taken again from the *Upanishads*, with their intuitive suggestions and ambiguities, which were the source of so much later thought.

> *This shining immortal Spirit*
> *who is in this Soul,*
> *and with reference to oneself*
> *this shining immortal Spirit*
> *who exists as Soul—*
> *he is just this Soul, this Immortal*
> *this Brahman, this All.*
> *Truly the Soul is the Lord of all beings,*
> *the King of all beings.*
> *As all the spokes are held together*
> *in the hub and rim of a wheel,*
> *so in this Soul all beings, all gods,*
> *all worlds, all breathing creatures,*
> *all these selves are held together.*[22]

REFERENCES

1 *Shvetashvatara Upanishad* 1, 1–2
2 *Brihad-aranyaka Upanishad* 1, 4, 7; 1, 4, 3; Plato, *Symposium* 189c
3 *Chandogya Upanishad* 6, 2, 1–3
4 *Brihad-aranyaka* 3, 9
5 *Ibid.* 2, 3, 1; *Maitri Upanishad* 6, 3; *Mundaka* 2, 2, 11
6 *Chandogya* 3, 14, 3–4
7 *Brihad-aranyaka* 3, 7; 2, 5
8 *Chandogya* 6, 1, 4–6
9 *Ibid.* 6, 10
10 *Shvetashvatara* 4, 1
11 *Katha* 2, 20
12 *Shvetashvatara* 6, 1

13 *Ibid* 3, 7
14 *Bhagavadgītā* 2, 72; 14, 27
15 *Ibid.* 15, 16–17
16 *Ibid.* 17, 23 f.
17 The *Vedanta-Sutras*, with the commentary of Sankaracarya, trs. G. Thibaut, 1, 3, 19 (p. 185)
18 *Brihad-aranyaka* 3, 7, 15
19 The *Vedanta-Sutras*, with the commentary of Ramanuja, trs. G. Thibaut, 1, 1, 1 (p. 130)
20 *Shvetashvatara* 4, 6–7
21 See M. Dhavamony, *Love of God according to Saiva Siddhanta* (1971), p. 168 f.
22 *Brihad-aranyaka* 2, 5, 14–15

5   Body and Society

All of this,
whatever moves in the moving world,
must be pervaded by the Lord.
Renounce it and then enjoy it.
Do not covet the goods of anyone.[1]

Matter and the Body

Indian philosophy and religion have often been regarded as other-worldly, pessimistic and even fatalistic, their concern being to get away from this evil world into the extinction or indescribable state of Nirvana. Such conclusions do not come from the main body of classical Upanishadic philosophy, or from the *Gītā*, or from popular Hindu religion. The theories of an indestructible soul, eternal Nature, and a universal Mind or God, do not necessarily imply renunciation of the world and the present life.

In fact the *Upanishads* teach a communion with the wholeness of existence in which matter and spirit depend upon each other and are bound up together. Brahman is both the formed and the formless, the mortal and the immortal. For the *Upanishads*, at least, the world is not unreal, since it comes from Brahman as a web comes from a spider out of itself, or as sparks come out of fire.

The unchanging element in the universe is described in various ways, sometimes as breath or spirit, sometimes as matter. In some remarkable passages Brahman itself is identified with food (*anna*), but this appears to be a natural religious materialism.

> *Whatever creatures dwell on earth*
> *are produced indeed from food,*
> *moreover they live by food*
> *and pass into it again at the end.*
> *For food is the chief of beings*
> *and so it is called the panacea of all.*

Those who worship Brahman as food
truly obtain all food.[2]

Food is the foundation of life, on which the breath depends, and on this depend the reason and the mind, leading to the highest joy and bliss. Or, as a later *Upanishad* and the *Gītā* said, the senses are high, but soul and God are higher. For the *Upanishad* quoted above, however, food is so important that it gives knowledge of the whole universe, and at the end the sage cries:

Oh wonderful . . .
I am food . . .
I am a food-eater . . .
I, who am food, eat the eater of food.
I have overcome the whole world.[3]

In somewhat similar fashion, in the famous illustrations of unity quoted in the last chapter, it is asserted that in the beginning there was Being alone, one without a second. This one Being wished to become many and so it emitted or divided itself into three basic elements: heat, water and food. These are the constituents of the universe. The human body is rooted in food, and through water and heat it is based in the ultimate Being.[4]

The relationship of body and soul are often discussed, from different angles. Although the body dies, yet it is the support of the deathless and formless Soul. The body (*sharira*) goes to birth, childhood, age and death, but it is the vehicle or chariot of the soul, which passes on to another body for further experiences. The body is the chariot in which the impassive soul rides, the mind is the driver, the intellect is the reins, and the senses are the horses, an image which Freud would have loved. Or the body is spoken of as a city with nine or eleven gates, which are the various openings in the body: two eyes, two ears, two nostrils, mouth, anus and generative organ; to these might be added the navel and the sagittal suture in the head.[5]

In some versions of Yoga there is a detachment and dislike of the world, which is opposed to the Upanishadic mystical partici-pation in the whole existence. But the *Gītā*, as will be seen, teaches forms of Yoga which despise extreme asceticism and give full play to life in the world appropriate to one's role in society. In some of the later *Upanishads*, however, as with the Jains and the Buddhists, there arose a pessimistic outlook which considered this world to be thoroughly miserable and evil, and the goal of life to be complete escape, both at present and after death. The later *Maitri Upanishad* speaks of the body as not only unsubstantial, but foul-smelling, composed of bone, skin, mucus, bile, tears, faeces, and so on, and it asks 'what is the good of the enjoyment of desires'.[6]

Buddhist literature gives further descriptions of the sad human state, which were intended to create in monks a disgust for worldly existence. The body was said to be composed of thirty-two im-purities, a receptacle of filth, with disgusting excretions from its nine apertures, like a drain into which refuse is thrown and, if it is so offensive in life, after death it can only be viewed with horror even by its friends.[7] Such attitudes were no doubt partly the result of preaching the ideal monastic withdrawal from the world, and also caused by the disease and heavy mortality of a tropical country.

It is perhaps significant that the idealistic non-dualism of Shan-kara also produced a poor opinion of the body, as compared with the unchanging immortal soul.

> *O you of deluded judgement*
> *abandon the opinion that the ego consists*
> *of a mass of skin, flesh, fat, bone and filth.*
> *Know that the true Self is the all-pervading*
> *changeless Soul, and so attain peace.*[8]

Suffering

The prevalence of disease in the tropics gave rise to concern with human and animal suffering. The first lines of the Sankhya text show that the removal of pain is a central interest of philosophy.

57

> *From the harmful effects*
> *of the threefold kinds of suffering*
> *arises a desire to know the means*
> *of removing it.*[9]

The commentators explained the three kinds of suffering as, first that which is natural and intrinsic, including bodily disease and mental infirmity. Then comes the natural and extrinsic, with pains derived from every sort of external cause. Finally there is the supernatural, which embraces the influences of heavenly elements, gods and demons. There were known material remedies for pain, such as medicine and earthly pleasures, but these were neither complete nor abiding. They did not produce that knowledge of the soul and nature, and the purification of the soul, which were both held to be essential to every serious person and spiritual athlete.

The Buddhists were even more preoccupied with the whole problem of suffering. The sight of sickness, age and death impelled the Buddha-to-be, and all Buddhas, into renunciation of the world, until the cause of suffering was found. Whereupon the saving message was proclaimed for the welfare of the world. The very first sermon attributed to the Buddha gives an almost medical analysis of the fact, the cause, and the cure of suffering.

> *This is the Noble Truth of pain:*
> *birth is painful, age is painful,*
> *sickness is painful, death is painful;*
> *sorrow, lamentation, dejection*
> *and despair are painful . . .*
> *The cause of pain is that craving*
> *which leads to rebirth,*
> *combined with pleasure and lust,*
> *finding pleasure here and there,*
> *namely the craving for passion,*
> *the craving for existence,*
> *the craving for non-existence.*[10]

This sounds like a pessimistic description of life, yet the teaching does not stop at analysis but proceeds to expound an Eightfold

Path of release by physical, mental and spiritual discipline. The ability to rise above craving and lust avoided the effects of pain, by a detachment which led to peace.

The way of the Buddha was first of all for monks, the experts in spiritual things and exponents of its doctrines, but Buddhism rapidly became a religion with a large following of men and women who regulated their lives by its principles. Great civilizations have been imbued with Buddhist teachings and their effects can be seen in the artistic productions of a great part of Asia. One of the noblest monarchs of all time was the Indian Buddhist emperor Ashoka, who in the third century B.C. gave a pattern of kindly government which has been equalled by few rulers anywhere or at any time. In the Edicts which Ashoka had engraved on pillars and rocks, numbers of which survive to this day, his benevolent work can be noted.

> *No living thing is to be killed or sacrificed . . .*
> *Everywhere two medical services are provided.*
> *These consist of the care of men and animals.*
> *Medicinal herbs useful to man and beast*
> *have been planted where they did not grow,*
> *similarly with roots and plants.*
> *Wells have been dug by roads*
> *and trees planted to shelter men and beasts . . .*
> *Officers work among the poor and aged*
> *for welfare and happiness.*
> *They are busy for the welfare of prisoners*
> *if they behave irresponsibly,*
> *and they release those that have children,*
> *or are ill or aged.*[11]

Buddhism is the most peaceful of religions, which spread gently right across Asia and into the Mediterranean world, despite hardships and persecution. It took Indian thought to the far east, gave literacy to Japan, and impressed its outlook on life on the art and literature of a great part of the orient. Buddhist morality was expressed in Five Precepts (Pansil or Pancha Shila), learned by

59

every southern Buddhist and these enjoin: compassion, honesty, purity, sincerity and temperance. A little book of verse called the Virtue-path (*Dhamma-pada*), which many Buddhists know by heart, teaches not only negative morality but more positively how to 'overcome evil with good'. One of the most popular devotional books of northern Buddhism, the *Path of Light*, prays that its follower may be 'a balm to the sick, their healer and servant', surrendering his own pleasures and being on behalf of all creatures[12]

The Jains also had a strong ascetic and monastic emphasis which led them to stress withdrawal from the world and its pleasures, though strangely they also produced great works of art and their temples are some of the most elaborate and beautiful buildings of India. The Jains have constantly taught reverence for life, not killing, non-violence, and were an important influence upon the life and teaching of Mahatma Gandhi. Jain temples in India today often have this text over the entrance: Non-violence is the highest religion. In their concern for life the Jains have not only respected human life, but also animal, and have had famous animal hospitals. An ancient Jain text declares:

> *Thus say all the perfect souls and blessed ones,*
> *whether past, present, or to come—*
> *thus they speak, thus they declare,*
> *thus they proclaim:*
> *All things breathing, all things existing,*
> *all things living, all beings whatever,*
> *should not be slain or treated with violence,*
> *or insulted, or tortured, or driven away.*
> *This is the pure unchanging eternal law.*[13]

Society

India has produced a succession of great civilizations which were imbued with religious ideals. The splendid architectural monuments of India and farther east are world famous, with their lavish and sometimes erotic sculptures which testify to delight in material as well as spiritual things. There have been great schools of painting and music, innumerable works of literature, and all the useful arts. Some of the greatest contributions of history towards culture and peace have come from India, and it is only the arrogance and ignorance of western racialism, militarism and technology, capitalistic and communistic, which fosters the notions that Asian cultures are inferior or that peace and freedom can be taken to the orient at the point of a gun.

Hindu social teaching is found chiefly in the moral and legal books, such as the *Code of Manu* and texts on the chief ends of man, some of which were begun before and others well into the Christian era. Three or four human aspirations were singled out, round which moral and social duties were grouped. These were: Virtue (*dharma*), Gain (*artha*), Pleasure (*kama*), and later a fourth added as Salvation (*moksha*). Virtue was a key word and Hindu religion is often called 'eternal virtue' or 'eternal truth' (*sanatana dharma*, the first word meaning ancient or traditional and related to our word 'senate'). Virtue included the duties of the classes of society, male and female responsibilities. Life was divided into four stages; those of student, householder, recluse and ascetic. To marry and bring up children was regarded as the normal and longest stage for all men, including priests, and retirement from the world came only after a man had seen his children's children.

Gain included not only the proper conduct of worldly affairs but the science of polity, the duties of rulers, state and international relationships. Kama (different from Karma, 'deeds') included all lawful pleasures, and there are priestly text books on the arts of sex such as the famous *Kama Sutra*. This book teaches many other arts than the purely sexual, discussing under Kama the arts of singing, flower-arranging, sewing, gymnastics, cooking, calligraphy, education of children, and so on. Salvation was the particular concern of religious and philosophical works, and it is more directly connected with our present subject of the soul.

Indian thinkers sought out the principles which would result in moral and social actions, assuming that the theory of a good life was important as well as the practice. A famous dialogue, given twice in the first *Upanishad*, states the principle that one loves things and people not simply out of human love for their own personality, but because of the abiding element within them, because of their very soul.

> *Truly, not for love of a husband is a husband dear,*
> *but for love of the Soul the husband is dear.*
> *Truly, not for love of a wife is a wife dear,*
> *but for love of the Soul the wife is dear . . .*
> *Truly, it is the Soul that should be seen,*
> *that should be heard, that should be thought about,*
> *that should be pondered . . .*
> *By understanding the Soul all this universe*
> *is known.*[14]

This has been called the high-water mark of ethical teaching in the *Upanishads*, and it shows how dominant for philosophers was the concern with the soul as the explanation and end of all that made life worth living.

The *Gītā*, however, is one of the most important religious manuals of right conduct and its abiding consequences. The problem raised in its first chapter, by the warrior Arjuna, is that by fighting he will destroy the order and classes of society, destroy Virtue in fact, and being filled with compassion for the combatants Arjuna lays down his weapons and refuses to fight. In his answers Krishna first enunciates the Sankhya doctrine of the indestructible soul, and then proceeds to assert that by failing in his class duty Arjuna is undermining the social system. It is the duty of a soldier to fight, though the concept of a just war is not discussed, or the problem of compassion as it might have been in a Buddhist text. However, to be fair it must be clear that the *Gītā* is dealing with the principles of all actions, and that the immediate battle-field is taken from the very first line of the poem to be a symbol of the Field of Duty.

The third chapter of the *Gītā* is chiefly concerned with the problems of action and is called Karma-Yoga. Karma, which is often misunderstood in the West as 'fate', is basically 'deeds' or 'action' and its results (perhaps related to our word 'create'). Karma was applied first of all principally to sacrifices and sacred actions, which were thought to be necessary for the survival of the world, and it came to be enlarged to include works in general. But because, in a world of cause and effect, action would not be isolated and its production of good and bad results entailed further activity, there was a tendency for some serious men to renounce action altogether and leave the world. India has had more than its share of spiritual athletes and has seen severe asceticism of kinds of which most of us have little knowledge and less inclination to practise them.

The *Gītā* severely criticizes those who imagine that by renunciation of worldly affairs alone they can attain perfection.

> *No one, for the shortest time,*
> *stays without doing anything,*
> *but each is made to act perforce*
> *by Qualities that from Nature spring.*[15]

The Sankhya teaching had shown that actions are worked in us by the three Strands which compose our Nature and so not even an ascetic is exempt from some form of activity. The *Gītā* remarks sarcastically that the holy man who sits and meditates may have given up some actions, but in his mind he is still thinking about sensual things and is rightly called a hypocrite. The way out for the virtuous man is to control his senses and, by being detached from hope of rewards, to do the work that is required for maintenance both of the body and society.

Many Indian reformers down the ages have opposed the artificial distinctions of caste, and the *Gītā* throws its way open to both sexes and all classes. But it stresses the importance of example from the highest levels of society, naming virtuous rulers who have acted for the proper order of the community. Even more significant is the divine example. God himself is not forced or motivated by the accumulated results of past Karma, and he lacks nothing so that he does not act from the motive of gain. Yet God is constantly at work in the world, for if he was not active the universe would dissolve into ruin, because men would follow the divine inaction. Society itself was established by God, since he both set the wheel of existence rolling and gave the rule for good conduct, and so man must be like God in his selfless activity.

A proper appreciation of action and inaction is necessary. It is not enough to act without thinking, or to renounce action altogether. The root of the entail of Karma must be discovered, and this is located in its fruits or results. There must be no carrot incentives or stick threats, no hope of heaven or fear of hell, love of reward or dislike of consequences. Action must be fully disinterested, done for the sake of duty alone, for the welfare of the world and the Dharma of society.

> *Perform your action as you should,*
> *or simply for the world's own good.*[16]

Detachment

To win that spiritual freedom (*moksha*) which all Indian philosophies regard as the highest goal, the chief end of man, the *Gītā* teaches a subtle form of detachment. Like God, the soul must be detached, while the body performs the duties imposed by its place in society. This releases from self-interest and, again like God, the detached man is not impelled by any Karma or any private gain to achieve, and so he can attain to the steady state of Brahman. It is admitted that this sublime attitude can be fully attained only by the few, and the wise man is warned not to disturb those who are of lesser understanding, but to encourage all other kinds of works while himself acting as a fully integrated man.

To reinforce this ideal by religious energy, the *Gītā* later proceeds to advocate not simply a negative detachment from results, but a positive attachment to God through love (*bhakti*). Its picture of Meditation-Yoga (in chapter six) requires solitude and self-discipline, but when the body is stilled the thoughts must be directed to the Lord and all man's integrated being absorbed in him. From then on the *Gītā* emphasizes love to and from God, and the peace that is found in communion with him.

The perfect man in the *Gītā* is one who has abandoned the desires that torment the mind, who is untroubled in sorrow and has lost delight in joys. Anger, desire and greed are 'the threefold gate of hell', those violent passions that figure on Tibetan Buddhist banners as the forces which destroy peace, and symbolized by cock, snake and pig. The man of steady wisdom has no desire for anything, in getting either good or evil, and neither delights in it nor loathes it. This does indeed seem to be unnatural or other-worldly, especially when later one is told to be alike to all men, the same to friend and foe. However, the *Gītā* often stresses one point and then compensates by concentrating on another elsewhere, and so it is also said that the integrated man who seeks the soul comes to look on all beings as in himself and himself as in all. Similarly God is the same to all, none is hated or dear to him, yet those who love him abide in him and he in them. So the wise man is kindly to all beings, including animals, since he is controlled and has the peace of Nirvana.

> *Their doubts dispelled by self-control*
> *the seers whose every stain is done*
> *delight in welfare of all beings,*
> *having Brahman-nirvana won.*[17]

Such doctrines do not mean that 'orientals' are less passionate or violent than the rest of the world, for the wars and communal massacres that break out now and again show how fierce human emotions can be. As the *Gītā* says, man is impelled against his will by desire and anger, arising from the dominance of the Strand of Passion, and this obscures knowledge and confuses the embodied soul. Similarly, peace and meditation are not the sole possession of the East, indeed in the conditions of over-population in our time these practices may be harder to achieve there than in the richer and more spacious living conditions which the West at present enjoys. But Hindu and Buddhist scriptures give ideals for conduct, which have been absorbed into the standards and mentality of Asian countries and will remain for centuries to come, even under Communism, and they well may outlive it.

The discipline of action (Karma-Yoga) in the *Gītā* is freedom

E   65 from the binding nature of activity, since one is not merely tied to present affairs. To act out of duty does not mean a blind or numbed performance of duty for its own sake, since action is contrasted with wisdom. Wisdom (*jnana*, like Greek *gnosis* and our 'Gnostic') is not just knowledge of ordinary things, the collection of facts, but it is the perception of eternal reality. The wise man has his actions 'burnt up in the fire of wisdom', since they are virtually abolished in it, as far as entail of Karma goes. Action is compared to a sacrifice which men used to offer to the gods with the idea of getting benefits in return, but the sacrifice of action is made in order to get rid of the bondage of results and this is perceived by wisdom. For wisdom is the great purifier, and as a fire reduces fuel into ashes so wisdom reduces actions into ashes. A man who is disciplined and integrated finds the truth of this in himself.

These considerations are vital for understanding the nature of the soul, here and hereafter. On earth the soul is connected with Nature, but in fact it is the Strands or Qualities of Nature that are involved in action and only a fool thinks that his real self is defiled by action. Detachment comes through realizing one's own separation from Karma and its entail. In the hereafter, the entail of Karma was supposed to be responsible for the lot of the soul in heaven and it determined the place of the final return to earth, as will be seen later. But the *Gītā* teaches the complete deliverance of the soul from the troubles of both present and future. Here the power of wisdom over works is demonstrated, for even the worst of sinners may cross over the sea of evil and rebirth by 'the ship of wisdom'. Later a similar saving power is attributed to loving devotion. Even if a very evildoer worships the Lord with single-minded devotion, he must be considered righteous because his resolution is right. This is very close to justification by faith, but it is not immoral, for that very love of God makes the soul righteous quickly and this man proceeds to eternal peace.[18]

Action, wisdom and love are all ways that are offered in the *Gītā*. Men differ according to their nature and needs, but these three ways are efficacious to all men for spiritual salvation. So man can journey through life, and the future life, detached from anger, desire and greed, and following the best way to God. The perfect man is one of 'steady wisdom', fearless and pure in heart, long-suffering and contented, kindly and loving.

> *Let man be free from self and I,*
> *not showing any being hate,*
> *patient, alike in pain or joy,*
> *both friendly and compassionate.*[19]

REFERENCES

1 *Isha Upanishad* 1, 1
2 *Taittiriya Upanishad* 2, 2
3 *Ibid.* 3, 10, 6
4 *Chandogya Upanishad* 6, 2, 3–4
5 *Katha Upanishad* 3, 3–4; 5, 1
6 *Maitri Upanishad* 1, 3
7 *Sutta Nipata* 1, 11
8 *Viveka-chudamani* 163
9 *Sankhya-karika* 1, 1
10 *Samyutta Nikaya* 420
11 First Major Rock Edict, see R. Thapar, *Aśoka and the Decline of the Mauryas*, p. 250 f.
12 Dhammapada 17, 3; *The Path of Light*, trs. L. D. Barnett, p. 44 f.
13 *Acharanga Sutra* 1, 4, trs. H. Jacobi.
14 *Brihad-aranyaka Upanishad* 2, 4; 4, 5
15 *Bhagavadgītā* 3, 5
16 *Ibid.* 3, 20
17 *Ibid.* 5, 25
18 *Ibid.* 4, 36; 9, 30
19 *Ibid.* 12, 13

6   Sleep and Death

Breath to immortal wind
and this body ends in ashes.
OM!
O Power, remember,
remember what has been performed.
O Power, remember,
remember what has been performed.[1]

Dreams and Dreamless Sleep

Sleep and death were both objects of observation and meditation, and their connection with the soul was discussed especially by the teachers of the *Upanishads*. The text quoted above is a prayer for a dying person who directs his thoughts to the supreme, for a merging of spirit and a memory of actions.

The state of sleep fascinated these thinkers, for in sleep one transcends the limitations of the visible world and one appears to be superior to death, perhaps because in sleep we may dream of those who are dead. It was said that there appeared to be two states of a person, one of being in this world and one of being in the other world, but that there was an intermediate state which was that of sleep. In the dream state one saw both the state of being in this world and in the next, with the evils here and the joys to come.

In subtle psychological analysis it was agreed that a sleeping man projects from himself the material of his dreams.

When one falls asleep he takes along the materials
of this all-embracing world,
he himself tears it apart, he himself builds it up . . .
There are no chariots there,
no teams of animals, no roads,
but he projects from himself chariots,
teams of animals and roads.[2]

This happens becauses the soul is a creator and in the state of sleep it is self-illuminated. There are no pleasures in the state of sleep except those that are created or projected by the soul, with delightful objects such as pools, rivers and lotus-flowers. The body and all that belongs to it is put to sleep, but the soul is awake and looks down on the sleeping senses, like a lonely swan which guards its nest but moves out of it at will.

In his later monistic philosophy Shankara said that just as in dreams the places and objects are unreal, so also in the visible world the body and ego are unreal and created by ignorance. The absolute consciousness had been clouded over by the mind which created objects of desire and notions of individuality and so it wandered ceaselessly in the enjoyment of the results of its actions. But this kind of idealism was not stated in the Upanishads.[3]

The *Upanishad* remarks that the sleeping body can be observed, with its movements. but the soul cannot be seen. It refers to the widespread superstition that one should not wake a sleeping person suddenly, in case his soul does not get back to the body in time; and it also refers to another opinion that the state of sleeping is identical with that of waking since the objects are the same. To both of these the teacher affirms that it is the light which inheres in the soul that is active in dreams, but it is not attached to what is seen there. The soul is like a fish swimming from one bank to another of a river, moving in both the dream and the waking state. But one should get free from desires and evil and be absorbed in the soul.

> As a man embraced by a loving wife
> knows nothing without or within,
> so this person who is embraced by the intelligent soul,
> knows nothing without or within.[4]

This comes about in dreamless sleep, the condition where no desires are experienced, as a falcon having flown around folds its wings and floats in the air. In that dreamless state the father is not a father, a thief is not a thief, a god is not a god, one is not followed by good or evil deeds, for he has passed beyond all the sorrows of the heart. In deep sleep one does not see, smell, taste, speak, hear, think, touch or know, and yet there is no cessation of the seer, smeller and so on, because he is imperishable. The seer becomes transparent like water, without duality, because there is no second object.

In a lively dialogue in the second *Upanishad* the nature of the true self is progressively explored. Prajapati, 'Lord of creatures', was teaching the gods and demons about the nature of the soul.

> *The soul which is free from evil,*
> *from old age, from death, from sorrow,*
> *from hunger and thirst,*
> *whose desire is the Real,*
> *whose thought is the Real,*
> *he should be sought,*
> *one should wish to understand him.*[5]

Indra who was chief of the gods, and a demon named Virochana, heard this statement and decided to look for that soul which would bestow all desires and all worlds. They went to Prajapati with gifts, studied with him for thirty-two years, and then asked for knowledge of that soul of which he had spoken. He replied that it was perceived in the eye, in water and a mirror, that it was the immortal and fearless Brahman. They both looked in a pan of water and saw themselves reflected, and the demon was satisfied and told his fellows that it was the bodily self which is to be served and made happy here. This materialistic doctrine is still the creed of demons.

But the god Indra realized that the bodily self can become blind, lame and crippled, and there was no final good in that. He returned to Prajapati, served him for another thirty-two years, and was then told that the soul that moves about happy in dreams is the immortal and fearless Brahman. But again Indra perceived the difficulty that although the dreaming soul does not suffer the pains of the body, it does experience unpleasant dreams and even weeps, as it were, and there was no abiding principle in that. Indra returned and served a further thirty-two years, and was told that the dreamless state, composed and serene, is the self, the immortal and fearless Brahman. Again Indra saw the difficulty that the dreamless sleeper does not know himself or things here, does not realize 'I am he', and has gone as it were to annihilation. So he went back again and served Prajapati for five years more. Finally he was informed that the body is mortal, but it is the support of the immortal and bodiless soul. When that serene one rises up from the body and reaches the highest light, it appears in its own form and is the Supreme Spirit.[6]

The Fourth State

A very short *Upanishad*, the *Mandukya*, analyses the self in a similar and even more elaborate fashion. The self has several states: the waking state which knows and experiences material objects, the dream state which knows and enjoys internal objects, and the dreamless state which is unified and full of bliss. Finally there is a fourth state (*chaturtha*, also called *turiya*) which is indescribable, yet this is the self which is to be known. This latter state is not that which knows external or internal, or a mass of knowing, not knowing or un-knowing.

> *It is unseen, incommunicable,*
> *intangible, undistinctive,*
> *inconceivable, indescribable,*
> *its essence of the conviction*
> *of the oneness of the self,*
> *the cessation of development,*
> *tranquil, benign, non-dual.*[7]

The last word gives the clue, for the non-dual (*a-dwaita*), the one without a second, is Brahman. As was seen in the chapter on Soul and World-soul, there is a strong Upanishadic tendency, though not complete or consistent, towards Monism or pantheism. This is the identity of Atman with Brahman, non-duality, merging into the Absolute. This short *Mandukya Upanishad* is the most monistic, seeing the true nature of the soul in identity with Brahman, that which has no elements, cannot be thought about or spoken of, and is non-dual. It declares bluntly that 'this Atman is Brahman'.

This *Upanishad* also states that the mystical syllable OM is this whole universe, the symbol of the soul and the totality of Brahman. The different parts of OM (or AUM) represent past, present and future and what is beyond them. The letters which comprise the diphthong and nasal sound are A,U,M, and a sound beyond. The three letters indicate the three states of consciousness in man, waking, asleep and in dreamless sleep. But the fourth state of pure unity is indeed the total undivided syllable, which is the one reality, Brahman and the true self. It is the fourth state beyond all others, it brings all evolution to an end, it is mild and without duality.

OM is held to be the perfect syllable, occurring as invocation and object of meditation throughout the Upanishads, and used as a text (*mantra*) for meditation by Hindus down to this day. It is the sound or word of the Absolute by which men come to knowledge of identity with the soundless and perfect. The *Katha Upanishad* says that this is the word which all the Vedas declare (rather an exaggeration), and that it is Brahman. The *Gītā* also says that OM is Brahman in one syllable, but then its strong theistic tendency brings it to declare the syllable to be the personal God Krishna, 'I am the one syllable of utterances', and the devout man should pronounce this word while meditating on God.[8] The monism of the *Mandukya Upanishad*, and some later Vedantists, has no basis in theistic works such as the *Gītā*. For the latter the soul, whether awake or asleep, is dependent upon the Divine Spirit but not identified with it.

Death

The first *Upanishad* has a number of thoughtful observations on death. In a tropical country many things take place in the open air, or in the company of a large family group, so that death is not private but fully watched. It was believed that there was a 'self in the body', like the 'subtle body' (*linga*) of the Sankhya teaching (see above p. 31), which suffered from the troubles of mortal existence. This was controlled by a 'self of intelligence', which mounted it like a charioteer directing a vehicle. When a dying man began to breathe with difficulty that was compared to a heavily laden cart creaking as it moved along. When the body became thin, through disease or old age, the 'person' (*purusha*, person or spirit) would free itself from the body,

> *Just as a mango, or fig, or berry*
> *releases itself from its stalk,*
> *and he hurries again to his entrance*
> *and place of origin, back to life.*[9]

In earlier chapters there had been a few suggestions that death was the end. A famous sage, when asked what did not leave a person when he died, said only that his name remained. And asked what happened to a person after cremation, he replied that it was a private matter, and with his questioner he spoke to him alone of Karma. 'What they said was Karma, and what they praised was Karma.' It is good or bad actions that form a man and, perhaps in a rather Buddhist sense, what seem to survive a man are his good and evil deeds.[10]

Later, man is compared with a mighty tree, his hairs being like the leaves and his skin like the bark. When a tree is cut the sap flows out, and when a man is struck the blood flows. When a tree is felled a new shoot springs from the trunk, but there man is different, for 'from what root could man grow up when he has been cut down by death?' A tree pulled up by the root does not grow again, and so when man is born, 'he is not born again, for who could beget him?' The text immediately adds that is it Brahman who is knowledge, bliss and the final goal, but although there is no textual evidence of dislocation, the tone of this sentence seems to be out of harmony with the first part of the section and may be a later addition.[11]

Questions about survival of death appear also in the *Katha Upanishad.*

> *There is this doubt concerning a dead man.*
> *Some say, 'He exists'.*

73

> *Others say, 'He does not exist'. . . .*
> *O Death, tell us this thing on which they doubt,*
> *What is there in the great passing-on?*[12]

For this *Upanishad* the answer is found in the indestructible soul, as discussed earlier, for it does not die when the body dies, since it is not born with the birth of the body. Post-existence, life after death, is certain because there is pre-existence, life before birth. The soul is primeval and eternal, it does not come from anywhere and has not become anyone, so that the wise one is not born and does not die.

The first *Upanishad* continues with its exploration of the problem by describing more fully the process of dying. When a man gets weaker the breaths or senses gather round him as he breathes with difficulty, like policemen and magistrates who assemble round a king who is leaving his realm. And as such officials and town leaders wait for a king who is arriving, with food and drink and lodgings, so all beings wait for a dying person saying, 'here comes Brahman, here he approaches'.[13]

When the soul is weak and confused, he gathers the breath together and his sight fails. 'He is becoming one, they say'; he does not see, smell, taste, speak, hear, think, touch or know. Then the point of his heart lights up, and his soul departs through the eye or head or one of the other bodily openings (see page 56 above). When the soul has left, life and the vital breaths also depart. 'He becomes one with intelligence, and what has intelligence departs along with him.'[14]

> *When all the desires*
> *that dwell in the heart are untied*
> *then a mortal becomes immortal,*
> *then he attains to Brahman.*[15]

The body lies dead and cast off, like the slough of a snake which is abandoned on an ant-hill. But the disembodied immortal life is Brahman indeed, and light indeed. The fully enlightened man became liberated and united with Brahman, and the stronger the belief developed in the fundamental union of Atman and Brahman, the more belief in the indestructible soul was strengthened. In theistic texts, like the *Gītā*, men were exhorted to fix their dying thoughts on the Lord, so that they could attain to his own state of being, for whatever state a man bore in mind at death he would grow into that state hereafter. Similarly the Buddhists of the Pure Land schools held that when a man was dying the Buddhas and other holy ones gathered round him and he would depart this life in tranquillity, to be reborn into the Buddha's Pure Land.[16]

Added to these beliefs, came the very powerful conviction of the transmigration of the soul from one embodiment to another, which will be considered in the next chapter. The first *Upanishad* hints at this, without much development, and provides a useful transition.

As a caterpillar comes to the end of a blade of grass and draws itself up on approaching another blade, so the soul when it has thrown away this body and dispelled ignorance, makes an approach to another body and draws itself together to enter it.

> *As a goldsmith takes a piece of gold*
> *to turn it into another more beautiful shape,*
> *just so the soul*
> *when it has thrown away this body*
> *and dispelled ignorance*
> *makes for itself another new*
> *and more beautiful form.*[17]

REFERENCES

1 *Brihad-aranyaka Upanishad* 5. 15; *Isha* 17
2 *Brihad-aranyaka* 4, 3, 9 f.
3 *Viveka-chudamani* 179, 254
4 *Brihad-aranyaka* 4, 3, 21
5 *Chandogya Upanishad* 8, 7–12
6 *Ibid.*
7 *Mandukya Upanishad* 7
8 *Katha Upanishad* 2, 15 f; *Bhagavadgītā* 10, 25; 8, 13
9 *Brihad-aranyaka* 4, 3, 36

10 *Ibid.* 3, 2, 13
11 *Ibid.* 3, 9, 28
12 *Katha* 1, 20 and 29
13 *Brihad-aranyaka* 4, 3, 37
14 *Ibid.* 4, 4, 2
15 *Ibid.* 4, 4, 7
16 *Gītā* 8, 5; smaller *Sukhavati-vyuha* 10
17 *Brihad-aranyaka* 4, 4, 4

7 Transmigration and Rebirth

To be born here and to die here
to die here and to be born elsewhere,
to be born there and to die there
to die there and to be born elsewhere—
that is the round of existence.[1]

The Travelling Soul

Belief in a survival of death is perhaps the oldest and most universal of the religious beliefs of mankind, and it is both accepted as an article of faith and reasoned by many arguments. But belief in the transmigration of soul, or Karma, from one body to another is especially Indian. It has been found only occasionally in European thought, and was taken from India to China and Japan by the Buddhist missionaries. The belief has flourished throughout India and the lands to which its religions spread, and it remained in reform movements that became separate religions, like the Sikhs. Transmigration is taken as a fact of life, though attempts have been made to prove its validity from memory, and more philosophically from the beliefs in Karma and the indestructible soul.

The English words to be used are important in defining the kind of belief that is held. Basically it is Transmigration (*sam-sara*, 'going through', undergoing a succession of states, transmigrating). This is the word translated 'the round of existence', or 'circling-on', in the Buddhist text quoted at the top of this page from *Milinda's Questions*. Another word commonly used in English is Reincarnation, but since the Buddhists do not believe that a soul is 're-incarnated' in the manner of Hindu belief, it is better to use the term Rebirth of their belief. This indicates a succession of states in which Karma is transferred from one psycho-physical organism to another. The same consideration applies to the use of the term Metempsychosis, which is derived from Greek and indicates the passage of the Psyche or soul from one body to another, in Hindu fashion.

Although belief in transmigration characterizes practically all the religions of Indian origin, yet it appears that it was not always so. It seems likely that transmigration was a fundamental belief of the ancient inhabitants of India, and was preserved by the Jains, Buddhists, Sankhya and Yoga Schools. But the Brahmin priests who composed the *Veda* hymns of the conquering Aryan people apparently knew nothing of belief in transmigration, and they did not mention it when they sang of death and heaven. The introduction to the idea comes quite formally and it is stated in the two earliest *Upanishads* in slightly different terms. The same young man who learnt from his father about the identification of the individual soul with the universal, was questioned by a prince.

> *Do you know where men go to from here?* . . .
> *Do you know how they come back again?* . . .
> *Do you know why it is that the world beyond*
> *is not full up?*[2]

When the youth confessed his ignorance he was told that he had not been properly educated, and in distress he returned to his father and complained. The father went to the princely assembly, and was told that this knowledge had never yet come to the Brahmin priests but was known only to the Kshatriya rulers. This suggests a difference between the priests who preserved the Aryan Vedic religion and the chiefs who included members of, and married with, older Indian peoples who believed in transmigration.

The dialogue continues by indicating ways on which souls go after death. Those who have knowledge and austerity rise up in the cremation fire to the divine worlds, and 'for these there is no return'. But those who practise ritual and useful works go up in smoke and arrive at the moon, there they complete the residue of their works and then return again into the space, smoke, mist and rain. They are born in plants and eaten by men. This mythical picture, not unlike the progress from dead to living bodies in the Yorkshire song of 'Ilkla Moor 'baht 'at', shows several elements of

Indian belief. Not all souls return to earth. The entail of Karma, where it is active, is carried to the world beyond. There is a double result, both in the life in heaven and in rebirth on earth.

Like a Greek belief, sketched by Plato in the myth of Er, the son of Armenius, at the end of the *Republic*, there is a strong moral element introduced into what might be thought of otherwise as a simply natural revolving of rounds of existence. Those whose conduct on earth has been good will quickly attain another good womb or birth, that of a priest, a ruler or a merchant. But those whose conduct has been bad on earth will receive an evil rebirth, in the womb of a bitch, a sow or an outcaste.[3]

This statement agrees with earlier ones which stressed the importance of actions (Karma), though there the point was suggested that Karma alone remained to be carried on to another life. It is clear on all accounts that,

> *One becomes good by good actions,*
> *evil by evil actions.*[4]

Karma is action and its entail, but it is not an unchangeable fate. It is accepted as the all-sufficient reason for the different conditions of men, the happy or sorrowful lots of this present life, but it is not unalterable in the future. Man is responsible for his own rise or fall in the round of existence. So belief in transmigration was a stimulus to action, since by good action now one might rise to a better condition next time, from a low or animal state to that of a man or a priest. On the other hand by doing evil man declines to an inferior or sub-human level, or to that of a mixed or outcaste, regarded as the lowest of the low.

The *Gītā* accepted belief in transmigration fully, since the soul is eternal, and this provided its first answer to Arjuna's objections to fighting in battle.

> *To the embodied soul in this body*
> *there come childhood, youth and age,*
> *and coming to another body*
> *does not confuse the steady sage.*

On one occasion Arjuna asked whether a man who practised Yoga inadequately, yet had faith, would lose both Yoga and faith and perish. But he was assured that no man who acts rightly can be destroyed either in this world or the next, for when he has reaped the rewards of his actions he will be born again into a noble family and will take up his struggle for perfection where he had left off.

> *There he wins to the unity*
> *that he had with his mind in former lives,*
> *from the position that he reached*
> *towards perfection still he strives.*[5]

Transmigration seemed to work automatically, as cause and effect, independently of any divine being. But the theistic writers could not exempt even this great natural process from the control of God. The *Gītā* has a great transcendental vision in which all beings are seen to be returning into the body of God, and a late classical *Upanishad* declares,

> *He is the maker of all . . .*
> *the cause of transmigration*
> *and of liberation,*
> *of continuance and of bondage.*[6]

Pre-existence and Liberation

Transmigration was believed to be very long, almost an endless process, and it fitted in well with belief in an indestructible soul. It suited either the dualism of Spirit-Nature in Sankhya teaching, or the virtual identity of Soul and World-soul (Atman-Brahman) in the Vedanta philosophy. It should be made clear, however, that belief in transmigration is not essential to the doctrine of the indestructible soul, which has other reasons to support it. If transmigration is rejected, as by a few modern Indian writers, or found hard of assimilation, as by many Western writers, the belief in the soul can remain unaffected.

Transmigration affirmed not only survival of death but life before birth, pre-existence. For if more than one life on earth was admitted, or more than one survival of death, then there appeared to be no limit to births and deaths. The life of the soul appeared to stretch away as infinitely before the present birth as after the present death. Like the universe, circling round in great eons of emergence, maturity and dissolution, so the soul journeyed in an almost endless round of birth and rebirth, death and redeath.

This constant transmigration has been compared to a wheel, in which the soul flutters about like a caged bird. Or it is a chain, where the soul is bound by the iron law of Karma which logically should admit of no deliverance from the consequences of actions until the full penalty has been exacted. Indeed the notions of supernatural deliverance, or forgiveness of sin, have been regarded as immoral, and contrary to the laws of cause and effect.

Even for the best of us the process of transmigration is long and wearisome. Those Western writers who toy with the notion of rebirth, generally anticipate just a few pleasant lives in which they would be rich and happy, like the lady who was sure that in her last life she was the beautiful Nefertiti, queen of the Pharaoh Ikhnaton. But since most people in most ages have had lives that were nasty, brutish and short, the probability of a painful rebirth is evident. The noblest of men passed through a series of existences lasting for millenia, according to the mythology. The popular Birth Stories (*Jatakas*) of the Buddha recount some 550 of his previous lives, in animal, human and superhuman existences, before he finally attained full enlightment and Nirvana. If that was so for the Buddha, how much longer would it be for the rest of mankind? So the *Maitri Upanishad* cries,

> *Please deliver me.*
> *In this cycle of existence*
> *I am like a frog in a waterless well.*[7]

Yet that there was a way out of the chain of existence was taught by all Indian religions and philosophies. Human transmigration, the microcosm of the universal macrocosm, need not follow the same endless round. For the law of Karma having been accomplished, the possibility was open for a better birth next time. Up from the level of a tiger, if one had been a moral tiger, progress was possible to the human level, and finally to that of a Brahmin or Buddha. This could bring salvation completely from rebirth, and deliverance from the round of existence to the indescribable bliss of Nirvana.

The *Gītā* offers several ways of liberation. The Yoga that it teaches is not passive self-discipline but activity, since the meaning of 'yoking' or 'joining' includes making effort and preparing for duty. It is of course activity detached from all desire of rewards, but by such renunciation of ego a man can purify himself and rise through successive births to becoming Brahman. This is Action-Yoga (Karma-Yoga).

There is also Wisdom-Yoga, said indeed to be the highest purifier. For, like the Greeks, the Indians placed great emphasis upon knowledge and held that the sage is the perfect man. Then his wisdom would make him free from the round of existence, when he saw through its shallowness and illusion. But the *Gītā* gives highest place to Devotion or Love-Yoga. Wisdom was hard and knowledge of the indescribable Brahman was rarely fully attained, though liberation might come that way for the few. But love is easiest and best, for men and women, of all classes. This love was from man to God, but also from God to man, and the theism of the *Gītā*, like that of the worshippers of Shiva, held that God would save his beloved from rebirth. Near the end of the *Gītā* comes a verse that is considered to summarize it all.

> *So abandoning all duties*
> *come for refuge just to Me*
> *have no fear, from every evil*
> *most surely I will set you free.*[8]

Buddhist Problems

It is not surprising that the Jains taught transmigration, and were perhaps the first to do so, since although they had no creator God yet a natural system of transmigration for endless souls was basic to their concept of the universe. What is remarkable is the tenacity with which the Buddhists held to the teaching of transmigration, and this illustrates the fundamental human need to believe in life after death. Yet not only did the Buddhists have no supreme God but they appeared, at least, to believe in no soul as well, so what was the vehicle or connection between lives and the nature of their transmigration?

The Buddhist dialogues are aware of the problems and treat them in their own way. King Milinda asked his monkish teacher whether there was any being that passed over from one body to another, and was told that there was not. Then if no being passes over should one not be free from the evil deeds of the past body? No, because there is a connection between one body and another. This connection, to show that that which does not pass over does reconnect, is illustrated in two ways. When a lamp is lit from another the lamp does not pass over but it reconnects. And when a pupil learns verses from a teacher the verse does not pass over but it reconnects.[9]

Vedantic critics of this view said that these were special illustrations, which did not compare with the passing of the soul from one body to another. But the Buddhists may have been objecting to the popular view which virtually identifies the soul with its bodily location since, like Nirvana, it must be unborn and uncompounded. Similarly in Sankyha teaching the Spirit is isolated and inactive, but it is the subtle body (*linga*) which transmigrates, and this gives a stronger reason for affirming that Karma is transferred from one body to another.

For the Buddhist the connection between bodies was Karma, for through the deeds done by the body (the 'name and form'), one reconnected with another body. The deeds followed the body like a shadow that never left it, though the deeds could not be pointed out as if they were located here or there. In the same way it is not possible to point to the fruits of a tree that has not yet borne fruit and say that they are here or there.

Transmigration is compared to a man who eats a mango and

plants the stone in the ground, another tree grows up and in time he eats the fruit and again plants the stone in the ground. In that way no end of the trees can be seen, for what is born here dies here and what dies here is born elsewhere. Yet while emphasizing the connection of deeds (Karma) between one life and the next it was very difficult to avoid using terms which imply spiritual connection. Milinda asked his tutor,

> *Does he who rises up know that he will rise up?*
> *Yes, sire, . . . when a farmer casts seed*
> *on the earth and it rains,*
> *does he know that crops will grow?*
> *Yes, he knows that.*
> *Just so, he who rises up knows that he will rise up.*[10]

Similarly, a man will know when he is not to reconnect with another body, and he knows this from the cessation of the conditions of reconnection. Just as a farmer does not plough or sow or store in a granary, and so his granary is empty and no more seed will be sown.

If monks had such difficulty in expounding and maintaining that there was no identifiable soul, the laity had far more. Recent detailed studies from Ceylon and Burma, two of the most conservative of Buddhist countries, have shown that the laity either ignore or reject the no-soul doctrine; and in funeral ceremonies which imply a continued existence in heavens and hells, rebirth or Nirvana, monks play a large part in all Buddhist lands.[11]

Memory

Buddhist teaching is negative, not seeing that a being passes from one life to another, but positive in asserting the reality of transmigration and Karma. But, like other Indian philosophies, Buddhism expounds its belief in accordance with its general principles and it makes no use, in the classical texts, of attempted proofs of rebirth from other evidence such as memory.

It is indeed remarkable that memory of past lives, which to

most westerners seems either to prove reincarnation by its presence, or disprove it by its absence, does not figure in the classical Indian texts. All those who believe in the indestructible soul regard it as natural that this soul will appear many times on earth, and they accept this as a fact of life. Like the Buddhists also they attach great importance to Karma, deeds, and the entail which determines future joy or sorrow.

Memories of past lives are not adduced as proof of transmigration, and though it is true that such memories are claimed in popular stories and circulate widely today, yet the theoretical foundation for the doctrine of rebirth did not originally depend upon such fallible and transient phenomena. For memory relies on the body which, even in mind and ego, dies and is not reborn. Only the unattached or indescribable soul, in Hindu teaching, is reconnected in some way with another body. Even for the Buddhists transmigration is in the order of things, immutable as cause and effect. In Buddhist lands many tales are told of people meeting again in another life, and remembering their previous acquaintance, but this requires a personal identity which is obscure in the classical Buddhist texts. In all the philosophies transmigration is regarded as a natural law which is beyond argument, and it does not depend upon memory.

The principal modification of the naturalistic basis to the belief comes in the theistic texts. The teaching of the *Shvetashvatara Upanishad* that God is the cause of transmigration and of salvation, has been quoted. And the *Gītā* held that the love of God would save his devotee from reincarnation.

> *And when their thoughts are fixed on Me*
> *then very quickly I am found*
> *their Saviour from the mortal sea*
> *that makes this transmigrating round.*[12]

REFERENCES

1 *Milinda's Questions* 77
2 *Brihad-aranyaka Upanishad* 6, 2; *Chandogya* 5, 3

3 *Chandogya* 5, 7
4 *Brihad-aranyaka* 3, 2, 13
5 *Bhagavadgītā* 2, 13; 6, 43
6 *Shvetashvatara Upanishad* 6, 16
7 *Maitri Upanishad* 1, 4
8 *Gītā* 18, 66
9 *Milinda's Questions* 71
10 *Ibid.* 73
11 See R. F. Gombrich, *Precept and Practice* (1971) M. E. Spiro, *Buddhism and Society* (1971)
12 *Gītā* 12, 7

8   Heaven and Hell, Ghosts and Spirits

The ritual-drinkers give Me sacrifice
believe the Vedas, seek for paradise,
and cleansed from faults they gain pure godly worlds
and taste divine enjoyments in the skies.

But having once enjoyed wide heaven's domain
their merit spent, the mortal world they attain;
so those who follow out the threefold law
desiring lust will come and go again.[1]

Temporary Heavens

There are heavens and hells in the mythologies of most Indian
religions, and some descriptions of them in the ancient scriptures.
But such lovely or fearful domains are not the final abode of
earnest souls. The monkish guide in the Temple of the Tooth in
Ceylon still points to the luscious paintings of celestial paradises
on the walls and says, 'Nirvana'. But every instructed Buddhist
knows that Nirvana is beyond all that art can depict.

The Vedic hymns spoke of the journey of the soul to the world
beyond and its arrival there. It had been carried up to heaven by
the fire of the cremation and on arrival in heaven received a 'subtle
body' in which it could enjoy pleasures like those of earth, but
without the inconveniences of this world. In heaven there would
be eternal light, cool winds, soft music, and refreshing streams of
honey, milk and wine; this is the usual furniture of oriental paradises, whether Indian or Persian, Arabian or Hebrew. There would
be plenty of eating and drinking, the pleasures of love, and reunion
with lost members of the family.

Heaven was said to be presided over by Yama, 'the restrainer',
who was the first man to die and find the road to the celestial world.
Later he became the God of the Dead and had two dogs, each with
four eyes or with spots above their eyes, who wandered among
men on earth as the messengers of death. In later epic poems Yama

judged the dead in the lower regions, the abyss or blind darkness. After its deeds had been read out the soul was sent either to the good ancestors in the heavens, or down to one of twenty-one hells. In the more sophisticated *Katha Upanishad*, as we saw before (page 30), Yama, as the lord of the world beyond, answered the questions of a young man who had died prematurely. These questions were about death as the end or the survival of death, and Yama affirmed the indestructible nature of the soul, 'it does not slay and is not slain.'[2]

Earlier *Upanishads*, as has been seen (page 78), speak of the souls rising either in the fire of cremation and going the 'way of the gods', from which there is no return to earth, or rising in the smoke on 'the way of the fathers' and coming back again in rebirth. It is curious that this rather primitive notion is repeated in the more advanced *Gītā*; those who depart in the fire, the day, the light part of the moon and the northward period of the sun, go to Brahman, while those who go at the contrary times come back to earth.

> *These ways of light and dark, they hold,*
> *are everlasting for the world,*
> *by one man goes to no return*
> *by the other to a new return.*[3]

A late classical *Upanishad*, the *Kaushitaki*, gives more details of the heaven to which the lucky soul goes. He arrives at the world of the gods where the creator god Brahmā welcomes him saying that he has reached the ageless river and he will not grow old. Five hundred nymphs then deck the man with robes and garlands and anoint him with perfumes. He comes to a lake and 'crosses it with his mind', and similarly with the moments and the ageless river. The soul shakes off its good and evil deeds, which are inherited respectively by his dear and not so dear relatives. He comes to a city, a hall, and the throne of Brahmā who questions him thus,

> *Who are you?*
> *He should reply . . .*
> *You are the Soul of every being,*

I am what you are.
He says to him, Who am I?
He should answer, The Real . . .
You are this whole universe.[4]

So one conclusion of the *Upanishads* is that beyond both the diversity of this life, and the many abodes of the heavens, there is the absolute Brahman. One who is freed from evil, who knows Brahman, the Absolute beyond the personal gods, goes to Brahman and becomes identified with that eternal being.

On the other hand it is in connection with the pictures of the heavens that the notion of the transmigration of souls first appears. There are many heavens and many gods, but these are all part of the cosmic scheme which will be dissolved in the course of the ages. Different gods have their own abodes, for example the warrior deity Indra rules over Swarga (related to our word 'solar'), the splendid abode of lesser gods and beautiful spirits. The heaven of the great god Vishnu was Vaikuntha, the 'irresistible', said to be on the great mythical mountain Meru, or in the northern ocean where Vishnu reclined on a great snake with a thousand heads, sleeping during the intervals of creation until the creator god Brahmā emerged again from a lotus in Vishnu's navel. But for the soul heaven was only temporary, although its stay there might last thousands of years. Yet in the end it would return to earth, as the verse at the head of this chapter says. Those who follow the Vedas literally, or perform prescribed sacrifices, will go to heaven and enjoy its pleasures, but when their merit is exhausted their desires will drag them down to earth again. Only rare liberated souls would go to the indescribable Nirvana.

Buddhist Heavens

In Buddhist mythology there are heavens and gods similar to those of Hinduism, from which they were largely derived. This shows that Buddhism is not atheistic, since there are many gods in its scriptures, though the Buddha is above them all. The gods are part of the round of existence and will perish with it, unless they can be reborn as men and finally as monks and Buddhas. The one who became the Buddha, the 'enlightened one' of this present eon, passed through many births and deaths, and visited the heavens as well as the earth.

An early text says that finally the Exalted One, as he was meditating under a tree, thought that he had not visited the gods of the Pure Mansions for a long time and at once found himself there. Several thousands of the gods saluted the Buddha-to-be and told him that it was a long time since the last Buddha had appeared. The previous Buddhas in their turn had decided to cease to belong to the host of 'the heaven of delight' and chose earth, and fit women of whom to be born. The pattern was constantly repeated and the descent of the next Buddha was prepared. Although Buddhism seemingly denies personal identity to souls, yet the Buddha could remember the details of the names and families of previous Buddhas, and at his enlightenment he recalled all his own previous lives on earth.

> *Thus through his clear discernment*
> *of the principle of the Truth,*
> *the Buddha (Tathagata) is able to remember*
> *the Buddhas of old, who attained final completion,*
> *cut off obstacles, cut down barriers,*
> *who have ended the cycle,*
> *who have escaped from all sorrow.*[5]

In a later text the Buddha-to-be has passed through many earthly lives, and arrives at the Tushita, the 'happy', heaven. Before he leaves there he makes four great surveys, of the time, place, continent and family for his last birth. Thousands of gods gather for his departure, surround his parents, and some assist at his birth which is attended with miraculous details though it is not a virginal birth. It is not necessary to say more, except to observe that the heavens and gods are transient, and yet they form a great part of popular Buddhist mythology.[6]

In the lush development of Mahayana Buddhism, the 'great

vehicle' of northern Asia, many supernatural figures were added to the Buddha, and many heavens. One of the most popular Buddhas is Amitabha or Amida, 'unmeasured Light', who is believed to dwell in the Buddha-fields, or the Pure Land in the western mountains. The Pure Land Buddhists are the most numerous of the sects, and they believe that faith in Amida ensures birth into his 'happy land' or abode of bliss. This paradise is described in glowing terms in popular texts. It is adorned with seven terraces, rows of palm trees, strings of bells, and enclosed with four great jewels. There are lotus lakes full of lovely water, lotus-flowers of all colours, heavenly musical instruments always playing, blossoms always raining down, while swans and peacocks sound the remembrance of Buddhist doctrine. Above all there are blessed Buddhas who speak the languages of the different Buddhist countries. And those who are born into that Buddha country are not there as 'the result of good works performed in this present life', but they come there by reciting the name of the blessed Amitabha.[7] Such pictures of the Pure Land inspired James Hilton to write of the bliss of Shangri La in the *Lost Horizon*.

Infernal Hells

Notions of a place or places of punishment for the wicked are very common and they are described in lurid detail. Naraka, a place of torment, is said in Hindu books to be divided into seven or twenty-one hells, and sometimes there are declared to be eighty-six pits in hell. The hells are below the surface of the earth, full of fire and instruments of torture, with which Yama has sinners punished. Lists are given in popular works of the various kinds of sinners in these hells, with their tortures, while the gods in heaven behold them. It is not unlikely that descriptions of circles and torments given in Dante's *Inferno* were derived from Islamic mythology, which in turn was influenced by Indian notions of an earlier date.[8]

The *Gītā*, which does not go into detail, speaks of the mingling of caste and the destruction of family laws which lead to hell. The three cardinal vices of anger, desire and greed are the 'threefold gate of hell'. And it seems that there is an eternal hell for cruel, hateful and base men. They are always cast back again into demonic wombs, and not attaining to the true God they fall down to the lowest way.[9] This is eternal punishment, but eternal must be taken in the sense of lasting throughout this cosmic cycle. At the end of the present eon all bound souls will be dissolved or merged into one, whereas those who are liberated go beyond the heavens to that bliss which is entire release from the changing round.

> *The undeluded man who knows*
> *the Highest Spirit here is Me*
> *knows all and then he fully shows*
> *with all his being love to Me.*[10]

The Buddhists continued the mythology of the hells as well as heavens, and there are many pictures showing the sufferings of the damned and tortures inflicted by devils. Temple paintings and scenes shown on Tibetan banners, which are in many museums, illustrate popular belief. The fires of hell (Niraya) are far worse than ordinary fires, and a rock the size of a house would be dissolved in a moment if it were thrown into hell. On the other hand, beings may suffer in hell for thousands of years without being dissolved, and this is due to Karma which continues its influence until the evil deeds are worked out. 'He does not do his karmic time until he comes to the end of each evil deed.' But once again, while sufferings in hell might be very long, they would end in cosmic dissolution.[11]

Ghosts and Spirits

Indian peoples, like most others, believe in the appearances of persons who have died, but in the classical texts such ghostly apparitions are never quoted as evidence for survival of death. In this the Indian scriptures differ widely from those modern Western writings which try to find support for belief in immortality in spiritualistic seances, in default of any more solid doctrine. The general Indian belief in the indestructible soul, as Death himself said, affirmed that the knowing self is 'unborn, eternal, abiding and primeval'.[12]

One Upanishadic text tells of a woman who was possessed by a Gandharva, a 'fragrant' spirit, a term sometimes used of the soul after death and before its rebirth. There were thought to be heavenly spirits like these who had a great partiality for women and exercised mysterious power over them. In this story it is a male spirit possessing this medium, and when he is asked his name he declares his tribe. He also gives knowledge about other people and the limits of the earth.[13]

Such tales merely echo popular beliefs of which, in the main, philosophical discussions take no notice. Beliefs in apparitions, possession and mediums have always been common in India, as in other continents, but they make no significant contribution to the theory of souls. Spirits may be manifestations of this transitory world, but they have no abiding value and certainly do not affect the ultimate destiny of the soul.

Heavens and hells, ghosts and spirits, play their varied roles in the cosmic round. But they do not profit, and cannot lead to salvation or eternal life. That is the role of Liberation, which leads to Nirvana and final bliss, to which we must now come.

> *Then must be sought the place to which men go*
> *and having found return no more below:*
> *'to that same primal Spirit I resort*
> *from whom this energy came long ago.'*[14]

REFERENCES

1 *Bhagavadgītā* 9, 20–21
2 *Katha Upanishad* 2, 19; *Gītā* 2, 19
3 *Chandogya Upanishad* 5, 10; *Gītā* 8, 24–26
4 *Kaushitaki Upanishad* 1, 5–6
5 *Mahapadana Sutta* 2, 53
6 *Mahavastu* 2, 1 ff.
7 Smaller *Sukhavati-vyuha* 10
8 *Vishnu Purana* 2, 5 f.

9 *Gītā* 1, 42–44; 16, 19–21
10 *Ibid.* 15, 19
11 *Milinda's Questions* 67 f.
12 *Katha* 2, 18; *Gītā* 2, 20
13 *Brihad-aranyaka Upanishad* 3, 3
14 *Gītā* 15, 4

9   Nirvana and Beatitude

This is the fixed state of Brahman
none is deluded who this attains
but goes to Nirvana of Brahman
if here on dying he remains.[1]

Freedom

The goal of Indian philosophy and religion is liberation or spiritual freedom, which comes from wisdom or works or love. This freedom can be attained in this earthly life, though that is rare, and in life after death it is beyond the temporary heavens and hells and the round of rebirth.

Spiritual salvation is release or freedom (*moksha, mukti*), liberation from clinging to or return to worldly existence, and so it is emancipation from the cycle of transmigration. But already in this world full control and integration of body and mind are needed, and release from those passions or qualities which distract the soul. So the *Gītā* says,

> *Controlling senses, thought and mind,*
> *the sage intent on full 'release'*
> *leaves lust and fear and wrath behind*
> *forever and is 'freed' from these.*[2]

However, there are great differences in the goals which are offered to the liberated soul in the various systems of thought. For the Sankhya and Yoga schools the aim is 'isolation' of the soul into its own unchanging essence, away from any contact with matter. So the *Yoga Sutra* says that the means of attaining removal of bondage is unwavering discernment which brings 'isolation of the Seer', And the very last verse of this short scripture defines this 'isolation' (*kaivalya*), when the Qualities of Nature cease to act and Spirit attains absolute freedom. Similarly the Sankhya text declares that separation from the body is obtained when Nature ceases to

95

act because her purpose has been fulfilled, and thus the Spirit obtains that 'isolation' from matter which is complete and eternal.[3]

This 'isolation' is of the self or soul, or rather of the countless souls which are self-subsisting monads. A similar belief is held by the Jains, who attribute the embodiment of the soul (*jiva*) in matter to Karma, and therefore they aim at its release from both Karma and matter. This release, in Jain belief, is into Nirvana, at the top of the universe, where there are many blessed and omniscient souls which are called 'isolated'.

The main stream of Vedantic Hindu thought, whether completely monistic or in some qualified sense, is quite different from the doctrines of the above schools. Here the souls do not exist in splendid isolation, but as joined to or identical with the Cosmic Spirit, Brahman or a personalized Godhead. It is this universal Spirit or Mind which is the cause, support and reason for the universe, and it is the goal and home of all the apparently individual human souls. The final destiny and freedom of the enlightened soul is not in an eternal perception of individuality and isolation, but in a merging of the self into the universal but conscious Self, which is Being-Consciousness-Bliss.

> *When a person is dying*
> *his voice goes into mind,*
> *his mind into breath,*
> *his breath into heat,*
> *the heat into the highest divinity.*
> *That which is the finest essence*
> *the whole universe has it as its soul.*
> *That is Reality. That is the Soul.*
> *That art thou.*[4]

Nirvana

Nirvana was a term used first by Jains and Buddhists and it was then made popular in Hinduism through the *Gītā*. The word Nir-vana means 'out-blown', put out, extinguished, calmed (*Vana* is related to 'wind'). It was used of a lamp or fire being blown out, and then of the flame of life and the fires of passions. Nirvana has sometimes, and unfortunately, been used in the sense of the 'extinction' of the souls, and it should be clear that this notion was never held by the Jains or Hindus. Like the Buddhists, they sought the extinction of all desires in the perfect calm of final bliss.

Buddhism certainly rejected the idea of continuing personalities, even though that might be held at the popular level, and it preferred to use negative terms about the indescribable Nirvana. There were, however, some nihilistic extremists in Buddhism whose views on Nirvana looked like extinction, and the great Buddhist commentator Buddhaghosa (in the fifth century A.D.) opposed such theories, declaring that while Nirvana is not understood by the ignorant it can be apprehended by the right means, 'for if Nirvana were non-existent it would follow that the right way would be futile.' Today, while some Western writers have treated Nirvana as extinction, there are no Buddhist schools in the East which maintain nihilistic views of Nirvana.[5]

The Buddhist *Questions* of king Milinda contain several interesting discussions on the nature of Nirvana. They begin by declaring that Nirvana is 'entirely blissful and unmixed with anguish', although the road towards it may bring anguish because of the renunciation of worldly pleasures. This is compared with the discipline necessary for establishing a kingdom, and the consequent bliss of sovereignty.[6]

The king asked whether it was possible to indicate the shape, size or age of Nirvana, by some argument or simile, and was told that this is impossible. For the amount of water in the sea cannot be reckoned, and the shape and size of spiritual divinities cannot be indicated. Yet it is admitted that there may be special qualities of Nirvana which can be demonstrated by similes. As a lotus flower is undefiled by water and mud, so is Nirvana unspoiled. As cool water allays fever, so Nirvana allays the fever of defilement and like water it quenches the thirst of craving for pleasures. As an antidote cures a disease, so Nirvana cures anguish, and it is sweet as nectar.

In a rather similar way in which the *Upanishads* spoke of the ocean of Brahman-atman (see page 45), so this Buddhist writer

G

97

says that Nirvana is like the sea, free of defilement, not filled by the rivers that flow into it, the abode of stainless beings and flowering with the abundant flowers of knowledge and freedom. Like food Nirvana sustains, strengthens, produces beauty, calms distress and removes exhaustion. As a wishing-jewel grants all desires, so does Nirvana.

> As a mountain peak is lofty, so is Nirvana.
> As a mountain peak is immovable, so is Nirvana . . .
> As a mountain peak is hard to climb, so is Nirvana
>   inaccessible to all defilements. . . .
> As no seeds can grow on a mountain peak
> so no defilements can take root in Nirvana . . .
> As a mountain peak is free from desires to please
> or displease, so is Nirvana free from them.[7]

It is perhaps not surprising, though not fully justified, that some Western writers have taken Nirvana to be the Buddhist equivalent of God, since it is perfect and transcendent. Yet, despite the above similes, Nirvana is only properly spoken about in negatives, and it is not that conscious Supreme Being that both orthodox Hinduism and other theistic religions have held to be essential to a doctrine of deity.

In Buddhist doctrine Nirvana is not past, present or future. In the typically negative manner of expression it is said not to have arisen, not to be not arisen, and not to be arisable. It is, in effect, beyond all description, definition, location and language. Yet Nirvana is not nothingness. There is indeed 'an unborn, unmade, unbecome and uncompounded', for if there were not then there could be no escape and liberation from what is born, made, become and compounded. 'But there is such an unborn', there is a way of liberation. This is the final goal of every Buddhist, and the special concern of monks who now seek freedom from rebirth or from the many heavens, and release into Nirvana.

Milinda's Questions make it clear that all men do not reach Nirvana, or not at present, but only those who know the truth and forsake defilements. Yet even those who have not attained to Nirvana know what a happy state it is, just as those who have not had their hands cut off know what a painful state it is by the cries of those who suffer. Similarly men know that Nirvana is happy, from hearing the words of those who have seen Nirvana.

The Buddha, of course, attained to Nirvana in a life on earth, the last of his mortal appearances after some five hundred and fifty previous births. At his enlightenment under the Bo-tree he attained Nirvana, and he might have left this world at once. But on the appeal of the chief gods the Buddha decided to stay on here, to teach the truth for the welfare of mankind. Forty years later he died or entered Pari-nirvana, 'full Nirvana', complete emancipation from births. So Milinda questioned whether the Buddha could be said to 'exist' any more, or whether he only existed in his doctrine. After a categorical answer 'Yes', the king was told that such speculations were unprofitable. For practical religion and in the ordinary uses of language, the Buddha remains supreme, teacher of gods and men, and as 'real' as Nirvana.[8] (See page 36 above.)

Final Bliss

Buddhist teachings about Nirvana have been said to give a minimum description of the meaning of liberation and to indicate a state of immortality, with negative restrictions on language. The *Gītā* follows on early Buddhism, using many of its terms and ideas, but freely adapting them to its own purposes. Since it is a thoroughly theistic book it is not surprising that the *Gītā* has its own version of Nirvana.

The *Gītā* coined a compound term, Brahman-Nirvana or Nirvana of Brahman, which did not appear in either Buddhism or the *Upanishads*. This is something more than the cessation of desires, mortal existence and individuality, which was taught by the Buddhists. It is also more than the 'isolation' of personal souls expounded in the Sankhya and Yoga schools, which the *Gītā* knew well. In the text at the head of this chapter 'the fixed still

G*

state of Brahman' means absolute peace, and progress to 'Brahman-Nirvana' is a liberation into that peaceful state.

In a later chapter the *Gītā* speaks of 'becoming-Brahman', which may still be language influenced by Buddhism meaning to 'become immortal', but perhaps with the added sense of union with the universal Brahman of the *Upanishads*. This is both a present and a future state, since the Yogi who has won to Brahman-Nirvana is said to 'delight in the welfare of all beings'. A few verses later peace is said to be attained by those who 'know Me' as the recipient of sacrifice and austerity, the Great Lord of all the worlds and the Friend of every being.[9]

The final state of the soul, liberated beyond the heavens and the cycles of existence, is bound together in the *Gītā* with its doctrine of the Highest Spirit, the Supreme Soul, the Changeless Lord. This being is God, revealed in his words and in personal relationships, though of course he is not restricted to personality since that is 'but a fragment of his glory'. The deity sustains the whole universe with a single part of himself and yet remains unchanged.[10]

The *Gītā* begins by using concepts from Buddhism and Sankhya in which God played no part. It speaks much of Yoga, which has a Lord but only as object of meditation. It also often quotes from the *Upanishads*, where there is the impersonal divine Brahman but little idea of a worshipful God and where the soul is virtually identified with the divine. It is the catholic yet original genius of the *Gītā* that weaves together different strands of thought, but turns them to its purpose of showing the loving relationships between man and God that are the goal of human endeavour.

In its early chapters the *Gītā* deals with the discipline of personality, the performance of duty in detachment from rewards, and the liberation that this brings. But chapter six achieves a deepening of thought, in which the integrated man, the Yogi, is in full contact with Brahman. He treats all beings as if they were in himself, and sees God in everything and all in God.

> *He himself in every being*
> *and every being in himself,*

he sees the same in everything
with Yoga-integrated self.

Whoever sees Me everywhere
perceiving everything in Me,
I never can be lost to him
and he is never lost to Me.[11]

The *Gītā* teaches love to God, not merely as one of the ways which can lead to liberation but as the very fulfilment of spiritual freedom. God saves his loving follower from the round of rebirth, and the world of creating and dissolving, and makes him enter into his very self. There is no doubt that his loving follower will come to dwell in God hereafter.[12]

The relationships of the soul and God are essential both on earth and beyond. The soul shares in the 'mode of being' or 'state' of God, and yet it is only a 'part' of God in the world of the living which becomes a 'living-self.' Liberation is certainly not an 'isolation' of the soul from all other beings. Nor is it a negation in which the soul, love and God would fade into vacuity. On the contrary, emphasis upon love brings a new concept of the final state of bliss as one of loving communion with the divine. The earnest soul becomes Brahman, attaining peace and immortality, but this is only preliminary to final beatitude.

The closing chapter of the *Gītā* depicts the integrated soul which has become Brahman, and is delivered from egotism, calm and free. Then having become Brahman, being the same to everyone, he finally attains supreme love to God.

And now he neither longs nor grieves
Brahman-become, with soul serene,
the same alike to every being
to Me he gains a love supreme.

By love he comes to know Me,
My greatness, who I really am,
and knowing Me as I really am
at once he enters into Me.[13]

Love of God

In this final state of the knowledge of God there is revealed the highest secret of all, which is that God himself greatly loves man.

> *The highest mystery of all*
> *My highest message hear from Me*
> *so I shall tell you what is good*
> *since you are greatly loved by Me.*[14]

Similar beliefs in the final destiny and beatitude of the soul in union with the divine Being, are found in the theistic schools of the followers of Shiva. An important text, partly based on the *Gītā* (the *Ishvara-Gītā*, 'the Lord's Song'), distinguishes three stages of spiritual progress. In the first, destruction of all selfish desires brings identification with Brahman. This leads in the second stage to pure knowledge and universal light. But in the third stage, the Yogis who know the truth enter into the most secret body of God which penetrates all things, and attain imperishable union with him. All ways of salvation are seen as finding their fulfilment in the supreme liberation, which is loving union with God.[15]

Other Shiva mystics sang at great length of the love of the soul for God, and God for the soul, often using sensual imagery in similar fashion to that in which Hebrew and Christian commentators on the Song of Songs demonstrated the love of God for Israel or of Christ for the church. Frequently it was said that body, mind and soul were merged into God and the self lost in him. But this loss must be taken in the sense of 'participation' (the root meaning of *bhakti*, 'loving devotion'). The goal is not extinction, whether in Nirvana or in a monistic identification with the Absolute. Egotism dies away, and in this life or beyond the mystic lives in God, doing his will and being utterly his own.[16]

The Vedanta Hindu philosophers sketched the progress of the soul according to their general outlook. Shankara said,

> *The state of final release is nothing but Brahman,*
> *and Brahman cannot be connected with different*

*forms, since many scriptural passages assert it
to have one nature only.*[17]

For the liberated soul there would be no entail of works, but also there would remain no distinction from other souls or from Brahman, because all are merged into the Absolute and 'everything is that Self.' After the death of the body there no longer exists any cause for rebirth, if the effects of actions have been 'extinguished by the power of knowledge'. Therefore 'the man who *knows* necessarily enters into the state of perfect isolation.' From this, it seems that monistic teaching holds out as final goal the merging of all enlightened beings into the neuter One, which is hardly distinguishable from the negative solitude of non-theistic Nirvana.

For the other great Vedanta teacher Ramanuja, the world and souls are not unreal, or just a passing illusion, they are a real part of the divine nature. Therefore God and souls will exist eternally, and the *Gītā* is quoted to prove that the Lord said, 'there will never be a time when we shall cease to be'.[18] Moreover, there is a sense in which personal identity remains, since there is a necessary distinction of subject and object, God and man.

> *To maintain that the consciousness of the 'I'*
> *does not persist in the state of final release,*
> *is altogether inappropriate.*
> *It in fact amounts to the doctrine—*
> *only expressed in somewhat different words—*
> *that final release is the annihilation of the soul.*
> *The 'I' is not a mere attribute of the Self . . .*
> *but constitutes the very nature of the Self . . .*
> *The 'inward' Self is thus the 'I',*
> *the knowing subject.*
> *This 'inward' Self shines forth*
> *in the state of final release.*[19]

Ramanuja goes so far as to declare that not only does the soul need God, but that God cannot maintain himself without the souls for they are his body. The relationship between them is one of love, for God is an ocean of compassion, and the earnest soul loves him beyond measure and receives the promise of abiding in him. In its final state, the liberated soul which is free from the bondage of Karma, has its powers of knowledge fully developed, and it has all its being in the supremely blissful intuition of the highest Brahman, the Supreme Spirit whose nature is absolute bliss and goodness.

> *We need not fear that the Supreme Lord*
> *having once taken to himself*
> *the devotee whom he greatly loves,*
> *will turn him back again to rebirth.*
> *For he himself has said,*
> *'To the wise man I am very dear*
> *and he is dear to me.'*[20]

REFERENCES

1 *Bhagavadgītā* 2, 72
2 *Ibid.* 5, 28
3 *Yoga Sutra* 2, 25–26; *Sankhya Karika* 68
4 *Chandogya Upanishad* 6, 8, 6
5 See Nyanaponika, *Pathways of Buddhist Thought*, 1971, p. 152 ff
6 *Milinda's Questions* 313
7 *Ibid.* 322
8 *Ibid.* 73
9 *Gītā* 5, 24–25; 5, 29
10 *Ibid.* 15, 17–18; 10, 41–42
11 *Ibid.* 6, 29–30
12 *Ibid.* 12, 8
13 *Ibid.* 18, 54–55
14 *Ibid.* 18, 64
15 *Ishvara-Gītā* 2, 52; M. Dhavamony, *Love of God according to Śaiva Siddhānta*, p. 93 ff.
16 Dhavamony, *op. cit.*, 168 f.
17 *Vedanta Sutras* with commentary by Shankaracharya, 3, 4, 52
18 *Gītā* 2, 12
19 *Vedanta Sutras* with commentary by Ramanuja, trs. G. Thibaut, p. 69 f.
20 *Ibid.* p. 771, and *Gītā* 7, 17

10 Criticism and Contemplation

For that is indestructible
by which this universe is filled
and This imperishable one
no one can ever cause to be killed.[1]

Doctrine and Argument

Indian beliefs about the soul and immortality which have been sketched in the foregoing pages have been held for many centuries, and they are maintained today with little change. This is not surprising and they are not necessarily out of date because of their antiquity. It has been said, with exaggeration, that European philosophy consists of footnotes to Plato. But in India there were not only ancient authorities, but a great variety of speculation over millenia. From Jainism and Buddhism, Sankhya and Yoga, *Upanishads*, *Gītā* and the Vedanta philosophers, there was a period of about two thousand years. There is ample material in the immense literature for many more centuries of discussion. That the doctrines are ancient does not mean they are out of date, any more than Shakespeare or Mozart are out-dated, for they have ageless qualities.

Yet in recent times the encounter with Western and scientific thought has brought some adjustments among modern Indian philosophers. Dr S. Radhakrishnan, a wide reader and charming writer, has tried to make a synthesis of the world's philosophies, but although some recognition is made of the reality of the world it is the monism of Shankara which dominates this writer's works. S. Dasgupta, who had an unrivalled knowledge of the Sanskrit texts and an acutely critical approach to the most sacred documents, was a deeply religious man yet he put forward no new dogmas; his value lies in his critical assessments. Aurobindo Ghose was perhaps the most original of modern Indian philosophers, and he propounded the ideal of the spiritual superman growing into the

Life Divine, and sought to bring all human activities into the discipline of an Integral Yoga.[2]

From a modern critical point of view the belief in transmigration appears to be the most vulnerable of Indian doctrines, but it has been taken so easily as a fact that it has rarely been challenged even by modern Indian writers. And yet it can be separated off from other doctrines and it may not be supported by clear evidence. It has been seen that traditionally it was not suggested that memory would prove the truth of transmigration. Reincarnation has been associated with belief in the indestructible soul, but it is clearly separable from that belief. The early Vedic teachers knew nothing about it, and the later Buddhists rejected the identifiable soul and yet held on to rebirth.

Reincarnation belongs rather to the idea of a cyclical progression of the universe, and of souls within that cycle. But again it is not tied to such a scheme, for Indian teachers held that the soul need never be reborn but could pass beyond the world-cycle to the bliss of Nirvana, to union with the supreme Being-Consciousness-Bliss. Nevertheless, despite critical difficulties, the notion of transmigration needs to be taken seriously, and it has had considerable appeal to Western peoples in modern times. When the physical components of our bodies are dissolved, they take up other forms, and so, says the Gita, it is with the soul. The soul cannot be destroyed, but it is associated with another form.

> *As when his worn out garments laying by*
> *a man some other newer ones will try,*
> *the embodied soul goes on to more new forms*
> *while putting off the worn out ones that die.*[3]

The doctrine of Karma has also been criticized in this century. As 'deeds' and their result the belief seeks to apply the facts of cause and effect. But whether the effect can be carried over from one existence to another, and even further can influence another life on earth, may be questioned. As an explanation of the happy or sad lot experienced by a man on earth Karma seemed to be a good theory, but it remained a theory and not a proved fact. Some men are born healthy and into rich families, others are born deformed and poor. While they may be responsible for their present deeds, it is impossible to prove that the state in which their present life began was the result of their previous activities.

Historically the doctrine of Karma has also conflicted with faith in divine grace and forgiveness. The *Gītā* plainly puts loving devotion not merely as an alternative to Karmic action, but as far superior, and God can save men from any evil who go to him for refuge. Pure Land Buddhism, the most popular branch of that religion, holds firmly to supernatural grace which responds to faith. Hindu theism, and the virtual Buddhist theism, demand a wider view of the relationships of human and divine than would be allowed by an iron law of Karma. So in understanding present religion, and future existences, the doctrine of Karma may at least need some modification.

It is the doctrine of the soul that is basic to Indian teaching, or rather the doctrines. That there is a mind or spirit in man is self-evident, and when Shankara said that 'self-existence is its own proof' he was anticipating the dictum of Descartes nearly a thousand years later, 'I think, therefore I am'. It is remarkable that many people in the West find difficulty in comprehending the incarnation of God in a man, and yet the world presents the daily spectacle of millions of minds incarnate in bodies which move about on the face of the earth. Indians had no difficulty with this, for the *Gītā* had said that to all embodied souls there came childhood, youth and age in the body.[4]

It seemed also self-evident that the soul was indestructible, since both God and men were believed to have existed always and would never cease to exist. The Westerner may question how the soul can exist apart from the body, to survive death or pass to another body, but to Indian philosophy the question was put the wrong way round. It should rather ask how the body could exist without the soul, for 'being cannot come from non-being', as the *Upanishad* says.[5] The most satisfying theories of the eternal soul were those of the Vedanta which viewed the soul as part of the divine being. The individual soul is eternal in the sense that it derives from the divine, and it is infinite also because it will come to final freedom in conscious union with the divine. Yet the soul, both individual and divine, is subtle and elusive and only perceived by rare minds.

> For one beholds him by a marvel rare,
> by marvel may another him declare,
> by rarest marvel one more hears of him
> yet hearing no one knows him whatso'er.[6]

Western Attitudes

Not only have Indian teachers been affected by Western ideas but the reverse has happened, and one of the most remarkable features of modern times is the revival and hitherto unparalleled influence of Indian thought upon the West.

On the one hand there is a widespread and uncritical acceptance of things 'oriental', 'occult', or 'esoteric', as if their virtue were guaranteed by an exotic origin. Pantheism, Karma, transmigration, Nirvana, and even magical notions such as levitation and third eyes, seem to be accepted without question. While this may testify to the need of the human spirit for belief, and for mythology, it also reveals ignorance of the profound differences of viewpoint which have existed within India itself for millenia. It is assumed, almost as an article of faith in some Western circles, that 'the Perennial Philosophy' must be pantheistic in the manner of Shankara and some passages in the *Upanishads*. The considerable modifications to monism in other *Upanishads* and in Ramanuja, and the clear theism of the *Gītā* and the Vishnu and Shiva religions, are ignored. Or, worse, the *Gītā* and similar texts are distorted to prove pantheistic theories.

At the other extreme is a more scholarly but radically critical evaluation of all Indian philosophy. Certainly not since the times of Shankara and Ramanuja have all Indian scriptures and philosophies been subjected to such critical analysis as today, and this is like a Reformation if not a Renaissance. Such criticism is right and proper, for a philosophy much more than a religion needs constant questioning if it is to survive. The critical and scientific methods of the West can do a great deal, both to purge Indian thought from outworn concepts and also to use it for a deeper spiritual interpretation of the modern world.

Unfortunately criticism is often only negative and, unlike Buddhist negations, it has no spiritual standpoint or goal in the light of which to formulate a working philosophy which is more than logic-chopping. Dasgupta, one of the most critical of modern Indian scholars, says in a study of Hindu mysticism:

> *With all my appreciation and admiration*
> *of the great achievements of the West,*
> *in science, politics and wealth,*
> *the Upanishad spirit in me may whisper*
> *from within: What have you gained if you have*
> *not gained yourself, the immortal, the infinite?*[7]

Different problems appear for members of the western monotheistic religions which are faced today by the apparent pantheism of India. And yet, as has been seen, Indian religions are not generally pantheistic, and their doctrines of God are complex and they have at least some similarities to Western teachings. But it is in the variety of ideas on the nature and destiny of the soul that India has made the most significant contributions to world thought. As was said in the first chapter, the monotheistic religions of the western world devoted their thought principally to God, and did not pay the same attention to the soul. Nowadays there is much confusion, and a striking neglect of teaching on the nature of the soul and on life after death. There may come 'light from the east', in an even more profound manner than it came to the medieval church through the heavens and hells which Dante borrowed from Islam which in turn derived them from India (see page 91 above).[8]

Contemplation

The Indian beliefs that have been outlined in this book are not generally dogmatic, they differ among themselves, and their theories may be adopted and adapted according to need. It is not necessary to claim that India had all the answers to the problems of human life, but at least in explorations of the mystery of the soul Indian contributions have been among the widest and most profound and they deserve the consideration of thinking men and women in all countries and in every age.

Most important of all, the soul and immortality are subjects for meditation. In India philosophy and religion were not separated, and thinkers were neither concerned only with theory nor simply with ritual worship. There was a great emphasis upon knowledge, but it was knowledge of eternal things and so was true wisdom. The goal both of the eightfold method of Yoga, and of the Noble Eightfold Path in Buddhism, was 'contemplation' or 'concentration' (*samadhi*). Taken up into the *Gītā*, this contemplation is a quietness and union with the true Soul.

Such contemplation, the practice of both philosophy and religion, is expressed in the theistic *Upanishad*. Developing an earlier statement that the soul is more subtle that the subtle, and more transcendental than the transcendent, it goes on to affirm that the vision of this great truth comes from divine grace. So in contemplation of truth, in the search for knowledge of the soul, the divine being bestows light and frees from sorrow.

> *Smaller than the small*
> *greater than the great*
> *is the Soul that is hidden*
> *in the heart of creatures here.*
> *One who is freed from sorrow*
> *by the grace of the Creator*
> *without the active will*
> *beholds the Lord in his greatness.*[9]

REFERENCES

1 *Bhagavadgītā* 2, 17
2 *See* S. Radhakrishnan, *Eastern Religions and Western Thought;* S. Dasgupta, *A History of Indian Philosophy;* A. Ghose, *The Life Divine.*

3 *Gītā* 2, 22
4 *Ibid.* 2, 13
5 *Chandogya Upanishad* 6, 2, 2
6 *Gītā* 2, 29
7 S. Dasgupta, *Hindu Mysticism* p. 168
8 *See* G. Parrinder, *The Christian Debate, Light from the East.*
9 *Shvetashvatara Upanishad* 3, 20; *see Katha* 2, 20; *Chandogya* 3, 14, 3

Index

eon, *see* Cycle
eroticism 60
eternal punishment 92
ethics 58, 61f.
evolution 15, 22, 28, 72
extinction 55, 97, 103

fighting 62
Five Precepts, Buddhist 59
food 55f.
forgiveness 81
four, aspirations 61
    eons 21
    stages of life 61
Freud, S. 56
frog in waterless well 81

Gandhi, M. K. 60
Ghose, A. 105, 110
ghosts 92f.
Gita, *see* Bhagavad Gita
God, as Mind 11
    Person 12
    Superman 12
    Creator 17f., 49, 110
    beyond Brahman 47f
    and souls 51
    body of 50, 80, 102
    active in world 63f.
    causes transmigration 80
    saves from 85
    beyond Nirvana 100
    union with 100
    love of 51, 102
    Sankhya views 17
    Yoga 17f.
    Jain 33
    Buddhist 33, 36, 83, 89, 98
gods, many 29, 41

goldsmith 75
grace 46
great word 44, 49, 50
greed 65, 91
guru, teacher 18

heaven 12, 87ff.
hell 12, 91ff.
Hill, W. D. P. 14
Hilton, J. 91
Horner, I. B. 38
Hume, R. E. 13

idealism 16, 57, 69
Ilkley Moor 78
illusion 49f.
immanence 42, 51
Indra, god 70f., 89
Inner Controller 42, 46, 51
Ishvara, Lord 18, 22
Ishvara-Gita 102
isolation 95, 99, 101

Jacobi, H. 67
Jainism 17, 18, etc.
    on creation 17
    soul 18, 32
    plural souls 28f.
    God 33, 83
    pessimism 57
    non-violence 60
    isolation of souls 96
jiva, soul, life 28, 32, 96
jnana, wisdom 66
justification by faith 66

kaivalya, isolation 95f.
kama, pleasure 61
Kama Sutra 61

113